# ODD MAN IN

A Comedy in Three Acts

by Claude Magnier

Adapted from the French
*Monsieur Masure*

by Robin Maugham

Copyright © 1958 by Robin Maugham
All Rights Reserved

*ODD MAN IN* is fully protected under the copyright laws of the British Commonwealth, including Canada, the United States of America, and all other countries of the Copyright Union. All rights, including professional and amateur stage productions, recitation, lecturing, public reading, motion picture, radio broadcasting, television, online/digital production, and the rights of translation into foreign languages are strictly reserved.

ISBN 978-0-573-01316-4

concordtheatricals.co.uk
concordtheatricals.com

---

**FOR AMATEUR PRODUCTION ENQUIRIES**

UNITED KINGDOM AND WORLD
EXCLUDING NORTH AMERICA
licensing@concordtheatricals.co.uk
020-7054-7298

Each title is subject to availability from Concord Theatricals,
depending upon country of performance.

---

CAUTION: Professional and amateur producers are hereby warned that *ODD MAN IN* is subject to a licensing fee. The purchase, renting, lending or use of this book does not constitute a licence to perform this title(s), which licence must be obtained from the appropriate agent prior to any performance. Performance of this title(s) without a licence is a violation of copyright law and may subject the producer and/or presenter of such performances to penalties. Both amateurs and professionals considering a production are strongly advised to apply to the appropriate agent before starting rehearsals, advertising, or booking a theatre. A licensing fee must be paid whether the title is presented for charity or gain and whether or not admission is charged.

This work is published by Samuel French, an imprint of Concord Theatricals Ltd.

The Professional Rights in this play are controlled by Eric Glass, 3rd Floor, 86-90 Paul Street, London EC2A 4NE.

No one shall make any changes in this title for the purpose of production. No part of this book may be reproduced, stored in a retrieval system, scanned, uploaded, or transmitted in any form, by any means, now known or yet to be invented, including mechanical, electronic, digital, photocopying, recording, videotaping, or otherwise, without the prior written permission of the publisher. No one shall share this title, or part of this title, to any social media or file hosting websites.

The moral right of Robin Maugham and Claude Magnier to be identified as author of this work has been asserted in accordance with Section 77 of the Copyright, Designs and Patents Act 1988.

## USE OF COPYRIGHTED MUSIC

A licence issued by Concord Theatricals to perform this play does not include permission to use the incidental music specified in this publication. In the United Kingdom: Where the place of performance is already licensed by the PERFORMING RIGHT SOCIETY (PRS) a return of the music used must be made to them. If the place of performance is not so licensed then application should be made to PRS for Music (www.prsformusic.com). A separate and additional licence from PHONOGRAPHIC PERFORMANCE LTD (www.ppluk.com) may be needed whenever commercial recordings are used. Outside the United Kingdom: Please contact the appropriate music licensing authority in your territory for the rights to any incidental music.

## USE OF COPYRIGHTED THIRD-PARTY MATERIALS

Licensees are solely responsible for obtaining formal written permission from copyright owners to use copyrighted third-party materials (e.g., artworks, logos) in the performance of this play and are strongly cautioned to do so. If no such permission is obtained by the licensee, then the licensee must use only original materials that the licensee owns and controls. Licensees are solely responsible and liable for clearances of all third-party copyrighted materials, and shall indemnify the copyright owners of the play(s) and their licensing agent, Concord Theatricals Ltd., against any costs, expenses, losses and liabilities arising from the use of such copyrighted third-party materials by licensees.

## IMPORTANT BILLING AND CREDIT REQUIREMENTS

If you have obtained performance rights to this title, please refer to your licensing agreement for important billing and credit requirements.

# ODD MAN IN

Produced at the St Martin's Theatre, London, on the 16th July, 1957, with the following cast of characters—

*(in the order of their appearance)*

| | |
|---|---|
| JANE MAXWELL | *Muriel Pavlow* |
| MERVYN BROWNE | *Donald Sinden* |
| GEORGE MAXWELL | *Derek Farr* |

Directed by HAROLD FRENCH
Décor by MICHAEL TRANGMAR

## SYNOPSIS OF SCENES

*The action of the play passes in the living-room of the Maxwells' cottage in an unspoilt part of Kent, near Romney Marsh*

### ACT I

SCENE 1  A Friday evening in Summer
SCENE 2  Saturday morning

### ACT II

SCENE 1  Half an hour later
SCENE 2  After lunch that day

### ACT III

The same evening
*Time—the present*

# ODD MAN IN

## ACT I

### Scene 1

SCENE—*The living-room of the Maxwells' cottage in an unspoilt part of Kent, near Romney Marsh. A Friday evening in Summer.*

*Two rooms have been knocked into one to make a charming living-cum-bedroom. There is a door back* C *leading to a delightful garden, and a door down* L *giving access to the kitchen and bathroom. A window* L *of the door up* C *overlooks the garden. There is another window* R. *The room is pleasantly furnished. There is a large divan with a loose cover thrown over it* R, *and a sofa* RC. *A rocking-chair is* C *with a small stool* L *of it. An oak dresser is against the wall* L, *and there are tables in the window up* LC *and* L *of the sofa. A radio receiver stands on a low bookshelf in the window* R *and there are further bookshelves above the window* R *and at the head of the divan. An armchair stands down* R *and an upright chair up* L. *There is a telephone on the dresser. At night the room is lit by an oil lamp converted to electric in a bracket on the wall* R, *and by table-lamps on the shelves above the divan, on the dresser and on the table* L *of the sofa. The wall-lamp and the lamps above the divan and on the dresser are controlled by a switch below the kitchen door* L. *The lamp on the table* L *of the sofa has its switch on the lamp. On the terrace outside the door up* C, *there is a white garden table and two chairs.*

(*See the Ground Plan and Photograph of the Scene*)

*When the* CURTAIN *rises, the only light comes from the lamp on the table* L *of the sofa, and the moonlight outside. The wireless is playing* "Someone to Watch Over Me". JANE MAXWELL, *in her pyjamas, is lying on the sofa, reading. After a few moments she looks at her watch, rises, crosses to the bookshelves down* R, *and puts away her book. After looking out of the window* R *for a moment she turns and looks at the telephone, then crosses and lifts the receiver.*

JANE (*into the telephone*) No, no, I'm so sorry, it was a mistake. (*She replaces the receiver, crosses slowly to the divan, picks up a cushion and unzips the cover*)

(*The telephone rings*)

(*She drops the cushion on the divan, runs down to switch off the radio, crosses to the telephone and lifts the receiver. Into the telephone*) Hello? Hello? (*She bangs the receiver rest*) Hello? . . . Well, my bell rang, but there's no-one there . . . Oh, thank you. (*She replaces the receiver, turns to the table* L *of the sofa, picks up a doctor's prescription from the tray, reads it, then picks up a small medicine bottle. She counts four drops into a glass, then changes her mind and empties half the bottle into the glass. She adds a small quantity of water, drinks the medicine and pulls a face*)

(*The telephone rings*)

(*She lifts the receiver. Into the telephone*) Hello? . . . Call from London. . . . Thank you . . . Hello? . . . Cynthia! Darling, how are you? . . . Yes, it's Jane . . . My dear, of course I'm pleased to hear from you . . . I'm so sorry, I was thinking of something else. How are things? . . . It's absolute chaos here—they've been painting our bedroom so we've had to move downstairs. They said three days and they've been at it three weeks. I'm not exactly on the crest of a wave. Do you realize that since I've been down here, Rupert hasn't been to see me once, he hasn't even telephoned . . . Of course he's not busy. Last year he spent weekend after weekend with us . . . Why shouldn't he get on with George? They went to the same school, didn't they? . . . Rupert and I? . . . No, strange as it may seem—we haven't . . . No, of course George hasn't noticed—you know George . . . Oh, he's all right. He's working in town and drives down for weekends. But I can't help feeling there's something wrong. Last time I rang I got a message to say he wasn't in . . . Listen, Cynthia, can you be an angel and help me? . . . Get hold of him somehow and tell him I simply must see him . . . No, not George—I can see my own husband, can't I? . . . Rupert . . . Yes . . . That would be wonderful . . . Do you know that it's got me so fussed I haven't been able to sleep—not a wink. . . . Warm milk? . . . Darling, tonight I've swallowed half a bottle of sleeping draught stuff . . . Yes—stuff to make you sleep; and I've a jolly good mind to swig down the other half . . . Now, don't worry, it's quite harmless . . . No, I'm not suicidal . . . Yes, yes, I will take a nice walk round the garden . . . Yes, and breathe in great gulps of calming fresh air . . . All right . . . George arrives tomorrow evening . . . No, of course he hasn't noticed. Darling, please phone me tomorrow morning and let me know what Rupert said . . . Please try to persuade him . . . Thank you . . . Good night.

(JANE *replaces the receiver, takes the glass and pours the rest of the sleeping draught in it. She is about to add some water, but changes her mind, puts down the jug and glass on the table and slowly exits up* C, *leaving the door open. The cuckoo clock strikes eleven.*

MERVYN BROWNE *appears outside the open window up* LC *and peers in. He carries his coat*)

MERVYN. Excuse me—excuse me—hello? Anyone at home? (*He moves to the open door up* C, *knocks on it*) Hello? Anyone in? (*He comes in, looks around, crosses to the kitchen door* L, *opens it and* calls) Anyone in—no-one at home? (*He turns, sees the telephone, puts his coat on the chair up* L *and lifts the receiver. Into the telephone*) Hello? ... Operator? ... Can you tell me where I am? I grant you it may sound a little odd, but I simply don't know ... Where am I phoning from? But that's what I'm trying to find out ... Oh, I see—yes. (*He looks at the receiver*) "Little Grittenden seven-five." ... Yes, seven-a-fife-a Lit-tel Gritten-den. It sounds perfectly delightful, but do you mind telling me where Little Grittenden is? ... Four miles away from where I'm phoning. That's a great help ... Now, do you know if there's a garage in Little Grittenden? ... Well, you see, my car's broken down. It won't go, I think it's gone on strike ... No, no, that was a joke ... There isn't a garage in Little Grittenden. Well, can you tell me where there is a garage? ... Dymchurch. That's splendid. And can you tell me how far it is to Dymchurch? You see, I'm a stranger in these parts, believe it or not. I tried to take a short cut and I seem to have ended up in Hampton Court Maze ... No, not literally. I was joking. (*He takes the glass left by Jane from the table and adds water to it*) Now, where had we got to? Oh, yes, I know. You were about to tell me how far it was to Dymchurch ... Eight miles! Now, my dear young lady, could you be awfully kind and get me that garage in Dymchurch on the phone? ... You could? That's just wonderful ... (*He drinks the medicine, looks in the bottom of the glass, then replaces it on the table*) Hello? ... Hello, are you the garage in Dymchurch? ... Thank heavens for that. Look, my car's broken down and I wondered if you could possibly ... Oh, you couldn't do anything tonight ... Not till tomorrow morning at the earliest. Couldn't you make a special effort? ... Oh, I see, telly ... No, I quite understand ... Walk? ... What do you mean, "It looks as if I'll have to walk"? ... Oh, you were joking. Well, I don't think it's very funny ... It's a cream and brown Bentley—convertible drophead ... It's about six miles along the lane from Little Grittenden, near an old barn, you can't miss it ... I suppose you'd better bring a tow rope ... P-R-X-seven-three-six ... That's right ... You promise you'll be there at eight tomorrow morning? ... Thank you. ... Good night. Have a pleasant evening. (*He replaces the receiver, moves towards the door up* C, *stops to yawn, notices the divan, goes to it, feels the edge, then sits on it, almost asleep. After a moment he lies down, kicking off his shoes one by one so as not to dirty the cover. His shoes fall on to the floor at the end of the divan. Then he curls up at the far side and falls fast asleep*)

(JANE *enters up* C, *closes the door, moves to the lamp, switches it off, then removes her jacket. She is so sleepy she only just has the strength to reach the divan. Without noticing anything unusual, she throws her jacket on to Mervyn's face, and flings back the divan cover so that it conceals Mervyn completely. Then she lies down on the divan beside the unconscious Mervyn and also falls asleep. Suddenly the peaceful silence of the countryside is shattered by the noise of a car approaching. Headlights sweep across the open window, the car stops, and the car door is opened and slammed shut.*

*GEORGE MAXWELL enters up C, carrying a suitcase. He puts the suitcase down up L, moves to the table-lamp L of the sofa, switches it on, then moves C and turns to the divan*)

GEORGE. Jane!

(*There is no reply*)

Jane!

JANE (*with an effort opens one eye*) Hullo, George! So you're back! (*She turns over and goes to sleep*)

GEORGE. Oh, there you are! So we're still down here, are we? (*Nettled*) I'm glad you're so pleased to see me.

JANE (*making a great effort to wake up*) What day of the week is it?

GEORGE. Friday. I came back a day early. I trust I haven't inconvenienced you.

JANE (*half asleep*) Of course you haven't inconvenienced me.

GEORGE. Thank you.

JANE (*her head falling back on to the pillow*) How are things?

GEORGE. Not too bad. How are you?

JANE (*going to sleep again*) I'm all right, thank you.

GEORGE (*sarcastically*) There's nothing like being welcomed with open arms.

JANE (*doing her best to follow the conversation*) Who's got open arms?

GEORGE. Never mind! I'm beginning to get used to it.

JANE. How are things?

GEORGE. Not too bad—you've asked me that once already. Can't you think of anything else to say?

JANE. I'm so terribly sleepy.

GEORGE. Then go to sleep, darling, go to sleep. I must say I am a little bit disappointed.

JANE (*trying desperately not to go to sleep again*) Why are you disappointed?

GEORGE (*taking off his coat and tie*) Because I've been away nearly a whole week and I hoped you'd be just a bit excited to see me again.

JANE. But I am a bit excited.

GEORGE. Oh, yes. But it just couldn't matter less. (*He takes off his shoes*) Do you mind if I sleep here tonight?

JANE. Of course I don't! What a stupid question!

GEORGE. I'm not so sure. One never knows with you.

JANE. What an old silly you are!

GEORGE. I can go and sleep in the room above the garage, if you'd rather. And you can have the whole place to yourself.

Scene 1    ODD MAN IN    5

JANE. Don't be a fool—there's plenty of room.

GEORGE. That's very kind of you. (*At that moment he notices Mervyn's shoes, picks them up and waves them in Jane's face*) And what may I ask are these?

JANE (*opening her eyes with an effort*) Shoes.

GEORGE. I can see that. But whose are they?

JANE. Whose do you expect?

GEORGE. That's just what I want to know. Whose are they?

JANE. I've no idea.

GEORGE. You've no idea?

JANE. No. None.

GEORGE. That's a fine thing! There's a strange pair of shoes in the house and you've no idea who they belong to.

JANE. Why should I know? (*She makes a desperate effort to examine the shoes*) They're men's shoes, aren't they?

GEORGE (*sarcastically*) Yes. They are. Unless you happen to have a girl friend with remarkably large feet.

JANE (*seriously*) I can't think of a single friend of mine with feet as large as that.

GEORGE (*with heavy sarcasm*) I suppose the postman left them?

JANE. Surely the postman wouldn't have left his shoes behind?

GEORGE (*livid*) Stop trying to be funny. Who do these shoes belong to?

JANE (*correcting him; sleepily*) To whom do these shoes belong?

GEORGE (*shouting*) Who? Who?

JANE (*leaning back on the pillow*) If you came all the way down here to make a scene, you'd have done better to stay in Town.

GEORGE. Look, Jane. I have in my hands a pair of shoes—men's shoes—I insist on knowing who—I mean to whom—do these shoes belong to.

JANE. You're becoming quite obsessional.

GEORGE. Answer me!

JANE. I'm beginning to find this shoe game a bit of a bore.

GEORGE. You're not going to get away with it like that.

(JANE *does not reply. She has gone off to sleep again*)

(*He shouts*) Where is he?

JANE. Where is who?

GEORGE. Your boy friend.

JANE. Which one?

GEORGE. "Which one?" Have you got a whole bunch of them?

JANE. Of course I have. But all the other ones go about barefoot. That's why you've never noticed them.

GEORGE (*beside himself with rage*) Do you think I'm being funny?

JANE. If you are, I don't mind telling you you're a complete flop as far as I'm concerned. Oh, darling, lie down for heaven's sake and we'll discuss it all in the morning.

GEORGE. I suppose there's room for me.

JANE. What precisely do you mean by that?

GEORGE. I mean that before I turned up tonight there was a man in here.

JANE. *"Was!"* But he's still here. Didn't you know? I thought we could all three doss down for the night together. Come along.

(GEORGE *creeps towards the kitchen door, listens, then flings it open and dashes into the kitchen. The crash of saucepans is heard off.*

GEORGE *returns limping and occasionally stopping to hold his foot. He limps above the sofa to* C. *All the noise has woken up* MERVYN *who sits up in bed and looks dazedly round at George.* GEORGE *sees Mervyn on the divan and can hardly believe his eyes*)

GEORGE. Oh! (*He tries to speak but words fail him. At last he succeeds in crying out*) Jane!

(JANE *does not stir*)

Jane! (*He switches on the remaining lights by the switch at the kitchen door*)

(*The room is now brightly lit*)

MERVYN (*tapping Jane's shoulder*) There's someone asking for you.

JANE (*sitting up drowsily without noticing Mervyn*) What's that?

GEORGE. Get off that bed at once, sir.

JANE. Why have you suddenly started calling me "Sir"?

GEORGE. Will you get off that bed, sir?

JANE. It's my considered opinion you've been drinking. (*She turns round, sees Mervyn, leaps off the divan, and throws herself into George's arms*) Who's that man?

GEORGE. "Who's that man?" "Who's that man?" Do you think I'm a complete half-wit? (*He shakes Jane like a terrier and drags her to the sofa*)

MERVYN (*nervously*) Do be careful, old man, you'll strangle her.

(GEORGE *lets go of* JANE *who sinks on to the sofa, and turns on Mervyn*)

GEORGE. You keep your mouth shut—if you want to see daylight again. (*He crosses to the divan*)

MERVYN. But really . . .

GEORGE (*seizing Mervyn's arm*) Will you get off that bed?

MERVYN (*getting off the divan*) I really must explain . . .

GEORGE. Shut up and come here.

(GEORGE *pushes* MERVYN *into the chair* C)

Sit down! I suppose you weren't expecting to see me?

MERVYN (*dopey from the drug*) No, I wasn't . . .

GEORGE. I'll give you a warning next time.
MERVYN. That's right.
GEORGE. Only there's not going to be a next time.
MERVYN. Yes?
GEORGE. What?
MERVYN. I mean, no.
GEORGE. Don't try to be funny with me. (*He looks at Mervyn menacingly and calls out*) Jane!

(*But* JANE *has gone back to sleep on the sofa*)

(*He shouts still louder*) Jane! (*He rushes across and drags Jane from the sofa*) You're not going to get out of it like that.
JANE (*opening one eye*) Hullo, George! So you're back.
GEORGE. Who is this man?
JANE. Umm?
GEORGE (*shaking her*) Will you kindly answer me!
MERVYN (*rising and crossing to George*) Listen . . .

(GEORGE *lets go of* JANE *who falls back on to the sofa, and turns on Mervyn*)

GEORGE. What's your name?
MERVYN. Mervyn Browne.
GEORGE. Right. I'm George Maxwell.
MERVYN (*holding out his hand*) How do you do?
GEORGE (*brushing away the hand*) This lady's husband.
MERVYN. I congratulate you.
GEORGE. Are you trying to make a fool of me?
MERVYN. No, I promise you, I . . .
GEORGE. Shut up! What were you doing here?
MERVYN. Sleeping.
GEORGE. Just get this, my fine friend. I'm in no mood for jokes.
MERVYN (*who can no longer stand up straight*) Why not?
GEORGE (*catching Mervyn by his sleeve*) No, you don't! (*He calls out*) Jane!

(*But* JANE *has gone to sleep again*)

Jane!
MERVYN (*joining in*) Jane!

(GEORGE *lets go of Mervyn, rushes across to Jane and lifts her up.* MERVYN *sits in the chair* c)

GEORGE. I'll wake you up if it kills me. (*He drags Jane across to Mervyn and forces her to look at him*) Well?
JANE. Good evening.
MERVYN. Good evening.
JANE (*to George*) You might at least introduce us.
GEORGE. Someone's going to get terribly hurt quite soon.

JANE (*to George; in a whisper*) Who is the man?

GEORGE. Mervyn Browne. Doesn't that ring a bell?

MERVYN. Mervyn Browne. Mervyn with a "Y", Browne with an "E". (*To Jane*) How do you do?

JANE. How do you do? (*To George*) Is he a friend of yours?

GEORGE (*shaking her*) One more crack like that out of you and you'll be sorry. (*He pushes her to* LC)

JANE. Do stop shaking me. I'm not a cocktail.

GEORGE. Are you going to explain or not? How did you get to know this man?

JANE. I don't know him.

MERVYN. Excuse me, but . . . (*He rises and moves to George*)

GEORGE. Shut up! (*He turns back to Jane*) How did you get to know him?

MERVYN (*leaning on George*) She doesn't know me.

(JANE *lies on the sofa and goes to sleep*)

GEORGE (*pushing Mervyn away*) She doesn't know you! You don't even know the man! That's the last straw. I suppose he was just passing by?

MERVYN. Precisely. That's just it.

GEORGE. So you were just passing by?

MERVYN. Yes, I was. (*He sits in the chair* C)

GEORGE. Right, we'll soon see about that. (*He crosses to the dresser, takes a revolver from the drawer, returns to* C *and waves it in Mervyn's face*)

(MERVYN *rises.* GEORGE *turns to* JANE *and waves the revolver at her, but she has gone to sleep.* MERVYN *sits in the chair* C)

(*He turns to Mervyn*) You must have had quite a party.

(*There is no reply. Both* JANE *and* MERVYN *are fast asleep.* GEORGE *fires a shot in the air.* MERVYN *and* JANE *wake up with a start.* GEORGE *turns on Mervyn*)

Go to sleep once more and you'll never wake up again. Get it? I'll shoot you down like a dog. You've been caught in the act—and don't you forget it. If I were in your shoes I'd mind my step. (*He turns to Jane*) And that goes for you, too!

JANE (*waking up*) Hullo, George! So you're back! (*She rises*)

(GEORGE *utters a stifled moan*)

GEORGE (*shouting*) That's enough! (*He flings Jane down on the divan and turns back to Mervyn*) You! What's-your-name?

MERVYN. Mervyn Browne. Mervyn with a "Y", Browne with an "E".

GEORGE. I know. You already told me.

(JANE *goes to sleep on the divan*)

MERVYN. My car broke down.
GEORGE. I see. So you went for help.
MERVYN. Yes.
GEORGE. And came in here?
MERVYN. Yes.
GEORGE. And you found my wife.
MERVYN. Not quite—you see ...
GEORGE. That was a piece of luck, wasn't it? You find a young woman all alone—with no other house near by. I know just what you thought ...
MERVYN. I didn't think anything. (*He crosses to the sofa and sits*)
GEORGE. Silence! I can see the whole set-up. You got talking. And you found out that her husband was away. "Splendid!" you said to yourself.
MERVYN. I didn't say anything to myself.
GEORGE. Will you be quiet? (*He turns to Jane who is asleep on the divan*) As for you! You ought to be ashamed of yourself. Within the space of an hour you allow yourself to be seduced by a perfect stranger. Charming! And there lies the woman who bears my name. (*He turns back to Mervyn*) As for you! I know just what you thought ...
MERVYN. I promise you, I thought nothing of the kind.
GEORGE. It never occurred to you I might come back a day early?
MERVYN. No, it didn't.
GEORGE. Well, it should have done. You should learn to think ahead—you half-baked Casanova! And how any self-respecting woman could fall for a dim-witted oaf like you simply defeats me.
MERVYN. Now don't let's lose our temper.
GEORGE (*brandishing the revolver*) And why shouldn't I lose my temper? Haven't I every reason to?
MERVYN. Do you know, if I were you I'd put that gun down. People sometimes do things they feel quite sorry for later.
GEORGE. If I shot you dead I wouldn't feel one twinge of remorse.
MERVYN. Now you don't really mean that.
GEORGE. Oh, so you don't believe me! Very well. You'll see. (*He moves threateningly towards Mervyn*)
MERVYN (*rising; hoarsely*) Think of that noose ...
GEORGE. I'd say you'd broken into my house. It would be manslaughter, at the very worst.
MERVYN. You're making a terrible mistake. (*He crosses to* R *of George*) Think of the scandal. Think of the headlines with a hideous photograph of you plastered all over the front page. I can just see the Sunday papers. Now aren't you glad I'm here? But for me you might have made a ghastly mistake.

GEORGE. Oh, no, my friend. It won't be my photograph on the front page.
MERVYN. Why not?
GEORGE. Because I intend to report your activities to the Police. I shall make a formal statement. And we'll see your pretty face on the front page—not mine.
MERVYN. I don't believe you'd do such a thing . . .
GEORGE. Wouldn't I? You'll see! I'm off to the Police Station right now. (*He gives Mervyn a push, Mervyn sits down abruptly on the divan*) You'll be hearing from me.

(GEORGE *stalks out up* C. *There is a pause.* GEORGE, *who went out barefoot, hurries back to collect his shoes. In her sleep* JANE *throws her arms round Mervyn's neck*)

Really! (*He dashes over to Jane and lifts her off the divan*)
JANE. Hullo, George! So you're back!

(GEORGE *drags Jane over to the sofa and flings her on to it*)

GEORGE. You thought I'd already left, didn't you? Right, I shan't go to the Police Station after all.
JANE. Why ever should you go to the silly old Police Station?
GEORGE. Joke away, sweetheart. Joke away. Drive me round the bend if you can. But don't forget the old proverb: "He who laughs last . . ." Remember? I got a bit over-excited just now, I admit I did. But I'm as cool as a cucumber now—and twice as dangerous.

(JANE *beckons to* GEORGE *who goes over to her*)

JANE (*whispering in George's ear*) Who's that man?
GEORGE (*with a wild cry*) Stop it, for God's sake! (*He walks around in circles*) I'm going to give you two a shock you'll never forget. If you think you can make a fool of me and get away with it, you've got a big surprise in store for you.

(JANE *and* MERVYN *both go fast asleep*)

You don't appear to be interested. Right. We'll discuss the matter in the morning. (*He switches off all the lights and sits on the chair* C, *still fuming with rage. He tries to settle down in various positions but without success. He glances enviously at Mervyn who is stretched out comfortably on the divan. After a while, he cannot resist it. He rises, crosses to the divan and lies down beside Mervyn*)

(MERVYN, *in his sleep, puts his arm round George's neck*)

(*He violently flings Mervyn's arm away*) Mr Browne! Really!

*The lights* BLACK-OUT *as—*

*the* CURTAIN *falls*

## Scene 2

SCENE—*The same. Saturday morning.*

*When the* CURTAIN *rises,* JANE *is lying on the sofa.* GEORGE *and* MERVYN *are on the divan. All three are fast asleep. The window curtains are closed and the room is lit by the bright sunshine outside filtering through the curtains. The cuckoo clock strikes nine. After a moment, the telephone rings.* JANE *wakes up. She is surprised to find herself on the sofa. She rises stiffly, yawns, moves to the telephone, and, still half asleep, lifts the receiver.*

JANE (*into the telephone*) Hello? . . . Oh, it's you . . . Yes, Cynthia . . . But what's the time, for heaven's sake? . . . Nine o'clock? . . . Yes, you certainly did wake me up. I slept like a log. That stuff I took is simply wonderful.

(MERVYN *wakes up*)

Do you know, I must have been so sleepy I couldn't even make the effort to go to bed. I woke up just now on the sofa. (*She laughs*)

(MERVYN *sits up and listens to* Jane)

What's more, I had the most fantastic dream . . . I'll tell you some other time . . . Darling, did you manage to contact Rupert? . . . And what did he say? . . . He's coming down tonight. But that's wonderful . . . Bless you, Cynthia. You've no idea what you've done for me . . . Yes, George will certainly be driving down . . . No, of course not. He'll be delighted to see Rupert. George gets bored stiff all alone here with me . . . Darling, I'll ring you Monday and tell you all. And—Cynthia—thank you . . . Ring you Monday . . . Good-bye. (*She replaces the receiver. She looks happy to be alive as she moves up* C *and opens the window curtains and window. She then crosses, opens the curtains* R, *turns and sees the two men on the divan. She gives a shriek of surprise*)

MERVYN. Good morning.

JANE. George! George! (*She shakes him*) George!

GEORGE (*waking up with a start*) Come in! (*He blinks up at* Jane) Oh! It's you.

JANE. Did you get back last night?

GEORGE (*sitting up*) I can't bear being woken up violently. You know that.

(MERVYN *is now sitting up on the divan.* GEORGE *has got his back to him*)

JANE. What's going on? Why didn't you put your friend to sleep in the room above the garage?

GEORGE (*who is the kind of person who needs at least half an hour before he is properly awake*) What garage?

JANE. Our garage, stupid.

GEORGE. I mean, what friend?

JANE. Wake up, for heaven's sake!

(GEORGE *turns and sees Mervyn*)

MERVYN. Good morning.

GEORGE. So you're still here!

JANE. Do you mind introducing us?

GEORGE. Now don't start that all over again. Give me ten minutes to wake up and we'll straighten the whole thing out.

JANE (*smiling pleasantly at Mervyn*) It looks as if I shall have to introduce myself. My name's Jane Maxwell.

MERVYN. Mervyn Browne.

JANE } (*together*) { How do you do?
MERVYN } { Hullo.

GEORGE (*to Jane*) Stop being social and get me some coffee.

MERVYN. I wonder if I could have some coffee, too?

JANE. I don't know how well you know my husband, but he's always a bit prickly before noon. You need kid gloves to handle him.

GEORGE (*trying to control himself*) Kid gloves, indeed! Get a move on with that coffee.

JANE. Of course, sir! Very good, sir! Right away, sir!

GEORGE. Just try irritating me this morning and see what happens. Just try!

JANE. You might at least make an effort to be pleasant.

GEORGE (*turning to Mervyn for sympathy*) Just listen to her. Now she wants me to be pleasant. That really is the limit.

MERVYN. Do be nice to her, dear fellow, or we shan't get any coffee. And I just have to have coffee—in the mornings.

GEORGE (*trying to keep calm*) Jane, would you be very kind and go and make us some coffee?

JANE. Please.

GEORGE (*sulkily*) "Please."

JANE (*ironically*) Sweetiepie. (*She picks up the medicine tray from the table* L *of the sofa*)

GEORGE. Oh, no.

MERVYN (*prompting him*) Go on.

GEORGE (*enraged but still trying to appear calm*) "Sweetiepie."

JANE (*crossing to the kitchen door*) There now! Do you see how much happier life would be if you could only try to be pleasant?

(JANE *exits to the kitchen*)

MERVYN. You know—she's got something there.

GEORGE. And I'd say you'd got the hell of a nerve. (*He rolls over and tries to sleep*)

MERVYN. Look, there's something I must tell you.

GEORGE. Not now. Later. You may not have noticed it, but I find it awfully hard to wake up in the morning. Last night you were sleepy. Now it's my turn. So be a good chap and leave me alone till I've had my coffee.

MERVYN. Why, didn't you sleep well?

GEORGE (*still controlling his temper*) Not very.

MERVYN. There's something you've got to know.

GEORGE. For the time being I know all I need to know. (*He tries to go back to sleep*)

MERVYN. You're going to get a big surprise.

GEORGE. Listen. I've had just about enough surprises to last me a lifetime. Now will you let me go to sleep for ten minutes?

MERVYN. I never went to bed with Mrs Maxtock.

GEORGE. Who's Mrs Maxtock?

MERVYN. Your wife.

GEORGE (*sitting up*) The name is "Maxwell".

MERVYN. Anyhow the point is that though I admit I did sleep beside her, I didn't sleep with her—if you get my meaning.

GEORGE (*controlling himself with difficulty*) My good sir, as you can see I'm perfectly calm and collected this morning. When we've had our coffee we can discuss the whole matter. In the meantime, will you kindly let me sleep? (*He lies down again*)

MERVYN (*getting up*) No. You've got to know the truth right now. You see my car broke down. I trudged for miles up this lane. This was the first house I came to. (*He stands* L *of the divan*)

(GEORGE *looks as if he is asleep*)

Are you listening to me?

GEORGE (*half asleep*) Umm...

MERVYN. I knocked on the door. No-one answered. I came in, and suddenly—I don't know what happened—I felt terribly sleepy and I just had to lie down.

GEORGE. Next to my wife?

MERVYN. Oh, no—no. When I lay down—(*he looks towards the divan*) your wife wasn't here. I swear it.

GEORGE. Are you suggesting that she came and lay down beside you and neither of you noticed anything unusual?

MERVYN. I can't think of any other explanation.

GEORGE (*sitting up*) Mr Browne, you must realize that it's highly improbable.

MERVYN. I admit that it's improbable. But I must ask you to believe me just the same.

GEORGE (*after a pause*) I suppose it's just conceivable that what you say is correct. I shall cross-examine my wife to find out.

MERVYN. Thank you, sir.

GEORGE. I only hope for your sake that it's true.

MERVYN. I assure you it is.

GEORGE. Right. (*He lies down again on the divan*)

(JANE *enters from the kitchen with a tray of coffee for three which she puts on the stool* C. *She has changed into a delightful dress*)

JANE. George! Coffee's ready.
MERVYN (*doing press-ups on the floor down* R) Coffee's ready, Mr Maxwell!
GEORGE (*getting up reluctantly*) Get me an Aspro, will you? (*He moves* C)

(JANE *looks at George without moving, then pours the coffee.* MERVYN *is still doing press-ups*)

MERVYN. I'm sure what Mr Maxwell really meant to say was: "Could you be an angel and please get me an Aspro?" (*He looks at George*) That was what you meant, wasn't it?
GEORGE. No.
JANE. That's quite different. (*To George*) I won't be a second. (*She moves towards the kitchen door*)
MERVYN. My dear young lady, I wonder if I could possibly have one as well?
JANE. Of course you can.
MERVYN. I might even take two. What about you, Mr Maxwell?
GEORGE. All right. Two.
JANE (*cheerfully*) That'll be four Aspros for the boys.

(JANE *exits gaily to the kitchen*)

MERVYN (*going on with his exercises*) I think your wife's enchanting.
GEORGE. What's that?
MERVYN (*lying on his back and pedalling in the air*) I said, I thought you had a perfectly enchanting wife.
GEORGE. I'll wait until I hear her version of last night before I agree.
MERVYN. Don't you believe me? (*He rises and moves to the sofa*)
GEORGE. I'd just like proof, that's all.
MERVYN (*exercising on the sofa*) My dear fellow, I'm deeply hurt. It's the first time in my life . . .
GEORGE. For God's sake don't do that. It makes me feel sick and I've a headache as it is. (*He sits on the divan*)

(MERVYN *does an "Arms-bend" as he sits in the chair* C.
JANE *comes in from the kitchen and hands coffee and Aspros to Mervyn and George*)

JANE. Here are your Aspros, George, here's your coffee.

(*Both men swallow their Aspros and sip their coffee.* JANE *takes her cup and sits on the sofa*)

(*To George. Conversationally*) How long have you known Mr Browne?

(GEORGE *is so surprised he chokes*)

GEORGE (*when he is able to speak*) I *don't* know him.
JANE (*in loud high-pitched amazement*) You *don't* know him?

GEORGE (*rising and bellowing still louder*) For God's sake stop shouting. (*He tries to control himself*) Whatever happens we must all of us keep calm. (*He turns to Jane*) Now then, just answer my questions.

(MERVYN *taps his coffee-cup with his spoon.* GEORGE *looks at him*)
MERVYN. "Would you be very kind and . . ."
GEORGE. And do what?
MERVYN. "And please answer my questions." You must be polite and pleasant when you speak to her.
GEORGE. Right. (*To Jane*) Now just tell me . . .
MERVYN. Naughty! (*He taps his cup again*)
GEORGE. Would you be very sweet and tell me—
MERVYN. That's better.
GEORGE. —what was the form when you went to bed last night?
JANE. What do you mean?
GEORGE. Answer me!

(MERVYN *taps his cup loudly*)
Will you stop that noise! (*To Jane; grimly*) Go on, I'm waiting.
JANE. Well, I hadn't slept well for some nights, so last night I drank half a bottle of some sleeping draught stuff that a nice doctor in Dymchurch gave me. I'd poured it all out into a glass and I was going to drink the whole lot but I thought I'd go into the garden for a breath of fresh air. So out I went. And I don't remember a thing after that till I woke up this morning on the sofa.
MERVYN (*triumphantly*) Now do you believe me? I must have turned up while your wife was taking a breather. Now I come to think of it, there *was* a glass and a jug of water on the table. I was so thirsty I just gulped it down. But the rest of your wife's sleeping draught must still have been in the glass, so I was completely drugged and I fell down on the divan fast asleep. Back comes your wife, also drugged, and lies down, too, without noticing any other foreign body.
GEORGE. You must admit it's the oddest bedtime story.
JANE. George, do you mind. (*To Mervyn*) So it wasn't a dream. You were beside me.
MERVYN (*politely*) Yes, I was.
JANE (*to George*) You'd never met this man?
GEORGE. No.
JANE. You found him asleep with me?
GEORGE. Yes.
JANE (*with rising indignation*) And you did nothing about it? (*She puts her cup on the tray*)
GEORGE. But, Jane, the thing was . . .
JANE. That's charming! (*She rises*) A fine man I'm married to! There's proof of devotion for you! (*She paces up and down* C)

(GEORGE *tries to speak, following her up and down*)

It's no good trying to think up excuses. I always knew you didn't love me. But I never thought you'd go beyond the bounds of common decency.

GEORGE. Jane, you've got it all wrong.

JANE. Have I? You find your very own wife asleep with a man you've never even met—and you don't do anything!

GEORGE. But I did—I shouted.

JANE. You shouted?

MERVYN. Yes. I promise you he did.

JANE. Shut up, both of you! (*She gives a bitter laugh*) You shouted! (*In a rage again*) And that's all you did—when you should have flung out the creature like the vile monster that he is.

MERVYN. Mrs Maxwell doesn't really mean that, you know.

JANE. Oh, yes I do! (*To Mervyn*) It's lucky for you that I'm not a man. If I'd found my wife lying next to someone I'd never even set eyes on, you'd still be in hospital. (*She turns to George*) And that's all you care for my virtue!

GEORGE. But, Jane . . .

JANE. I suppose I ought to have known by now. My virtue means nothing to you.

MERVYN. But he's just told you . . .

JANE. He's told me nothing of the sort. I'm still waiting for his explanation.

MERVYN. Mr Maxwell—your turn.

GEORGE (*staring blankly at Mervyn*) What's that?

MERVYN. Your turn to explain.

GEORGE (*in amazement*) Explain? Explain what?

MERVYN. Your incredible behaviour. (*He puts his cup on the stool*)

GEORGE. Well that really is the limit!

JANE. That's right. Think up any old excuse between you. But don't make the mistake of thinking I'll believe a word you say.

GEORGE. I've had enough. I'm the one who should be in a rage—not you! (*He puts his cup on the stool*)

JANE. That's the whole point. I'm furious because you're not.

GEORGE (*sitting on the divan*) Oh, my head! (*He clasps his head in his hands*)

MERVYN (*handing George the bottle of Aspros*) Here, have an Aspro.

GEORGE (*taking it*) Thanks.

JANE (*to Mervyn*) Leave the room.

MERVYN. I beg your pardon?

JANE. I said leave the room.

MERVYN. I don't want to . . .

JANE (*picking up the revolver and pointing it at Mervyn*) We'll see about that.

(MERVYN *raises his hands above his head and stands up*. JANE *advances towards Mervyn who withdraws down* LC)

GEORGE. Oh, no, Jane, no.
JANE. I'm going to count up to three. And if you're not out of this house by the time I reach *three* I shall pull the trigger. *One* . . .
GEORGE (*rising*) Jane, put that gun down at once.
MERVYN. Mr Maxwell's quite right.
JANE. Frightened?
MERVYN. Practically to death. (*To George*) Wouldn't you be? Just put yourself in my place.
GEORGE. I'm all right where I am, thanks.
JANE. Two.
MERVYN. It's your plain duty to tell your wife to drop that gun at once.
GEORGE (*nervously*) Jane, dear, would you be very sweet and . . .
JANE (*swinging round suddenly and pointing the gun at George*) One more word out of you and you'll be the first to go.
MERVYN. Mr Maxwell, do something.
GEORGE. How can I? You know damn well if I do she'll shoot me first.
MERVYN. Why not risk it?
JANE. Two and a half . . .
MERVYN. Have you pulled back the safety-catch?
JANE. What safety-catch?
MERVYN (*pointing to it*) That little knob.
JANE (*looking at the revolver*) What little knob?
MERVYN (*moving cautiously towards her*) That little knob round there on the side—there—I'll show you.

(MERVYN *seizes the revolver.* JANE *struggles with him. The gun goes off.* JANE *falls into* MERVYN'S *arms in a dead faint.* GEORGE *rushes up to them*)

GEORGE. Jane!
MERVYN. Is she hurt?
GEORGE (*feeling her pulse*) Just fainted. I think.
MERVYN. Good.

(*They help Jane into the chair* C. GEORGE *pats her hands*)

GEORGE. That will show you how dangerous it is to play about with firearms.
JANE (*coming round*) Where am I?
MERVYN. Four miles from Little Grittenden.
JANE. So you're still here?
MERVYN. Yes—thanks to the grace of Providence. But I had a narrow escape. (*To George*) Have you got some brandy?
GEORGE. Do you think she needs it?
MERVYN. Not her—me.
GEORGE. All right, I'll get some. (*He stops patting Jane's hands*

*and gives them to Mervyn*) Here, you take over. (*He crosses to* R *and pours two glasses of brandy*)

(MERVYN *begins patting Jane's hands as George did, but then starts to stroke them.* JANE *gives him a sharp slap*)

GEORGE (*handing Mervyn a glass*) A good snort will pull us together.

MERVYN (*raising his glass*) Let's drink to Mrs Maxwell's health.

GEORGE. Yes, jolly good luck.

(MERVYN *and* GEORGE *touch glasses and drink*)

GEORGE. That's better.

JANE. Well, now the joke's over.

MERVYN. So you were pretending all the time?

GEORGE (*laughing idiotically*) Of course she was. She wasn't really cross. Were you, sweetheart?

JANE (*loudly*) George!

(GEORGE *stops laughing*)

GEORGE. Yes, dear?

JANE. Throw this man out!

GEORGE (*nervously*) Yes, dear, of course. Straight away. (*He takes the glass from Mervyn's hand*) Where's your car? (*He puts the glasses on the tray* R)

MERVYN. Down the lane about two miles.

GEORGE. I'll get our car out of the garage and drive you there. Otherwise we'll have the same trouble all over again. (*He crosses to the door up* C)

MERVYN. That's extremely kind of you.

(GEORGE *exits up* C)

JANE. Get your coat.

(*The sound of a car starting is heard off*)

MERVYN (*collecting his coat*) There's one thing I would like to say.

JANE. Put it on.

MERVYN (*putting on his coat*) Mrs Maxwell . . .

(GEORGE *enters up* C)

GEORGE. She's always a bit cold to start with.

MERVYN. I beg your pardon.

GEORGE. Just have to keep at it. She soon warms up. Takes about five minutes.

(GEORGE *exits up* C)

MERVYN. May I finish my coffee?

JANE (*moving below the sofa*) If you want to.
MERVYN (*picking up his coffee*) So you don't remember anything?
JANE. I've already said I didn't.
MERVYN (*sadly*) You're lucky.
JANE. Why?
MERVYN. Because I shall always think of you. Because I shall mind leaving you so terribly.
JANE. Don't be ridiculous!
MERVYN (*enigmatically*) Of course, you wouldn't understand. (*He drinks his coffee and puts the cup on the stool*)
JANE. There's nothing *to* understand. We don't know each other. And you'll go on your own way as if we'd never met.
MERVYN. How fantastic it all is when you come to think of it. I've come into your life but you'll never remember it.
JANE. Don't exaggerate. You never came into my life.
MERVYN. Oh, well! Perhaps it's better you should never know.
JANE. Never know what?
MERVYN (*dramatically*) Don't ask me. I promise you it's better as it is.
JANE. There's no need to be so mysterious.
MERVYN. Far better. I shall be leaving you in a few moments but I can't help feeling slightly bitter. When I think of those two glorious hours . . .
JANE. What glorious hours?
MERVYN. Forgive me. I've said too much already. And I did so hope you'd never find out.
JANE. Never find out what?
MERVYN. Do you mean really you don't remember anything? Not a single thing?
JANE. What should I remember?
MERVYN (*pretending to be embarrassed*) Nothing much.
JANE (*beginning to get irritated*) Have it your own way. If you don't want to tell me, then don't. Good-bye, Mr Browne.
MERVYN. But I'll promise you this. Your husband will never know.
JANE. My husband!
MERVYN. Far better not.
JANE (*a little worried*) Just what are you trying to insinuate?
MERVYN. It's no good. I can't bear it a moment longer. I must tell you. Last night before your husband came in . . .
JANE. Yes?
MERVYN. No—I simply can't say it.
JANE. Have you got the impudence to suggest . . .?
MERVYN. Alas, I am not suggesting. I'm stating a plain fact.
JANE. You took advantage . . .
MERVYN. No, don't think that for an instant. If I'd thought for one moment that you weren't quite yourself, you'd have every

right to fling me out of your house. But you see I didn't notice a thing.

JANE. You took . . .

MERVYN (*very gently*) No, I must be brutally frank. I didn't take anything. No. The boot was on the other . . . *You* took.

JANE. What?

MERVYN. That's to say . . .

JANE. How appalling!

MERVYN. Oh, I won't say that.

JANE. Then you should do.

MERVYN. I suppose I should have struggled.

JANE. I don't believe it.

MERVYN. You mean I shouldn't have struggled?

JANE. I mean I don't believe a word of all this.

MERVYN. You don't have to.

JANE. Surely I would have noticed something was going on?

MERVYN. I know—it's your loss of memory that's so terribly worrying. You see, last night you seemed to notice everything.

JANE. But you drank as much of the stuff as I did.

MERVYN (*moving to R of Jane*) I only told your husband that to calm him down. Now I come to think of it I reckon you must have drunk the whole bottle yourself. I don't remember drinking anything.

JANE. Oh, how ghastly.

MERVYN (*taking her hand*) Jane. Jane, my little darling.

JANE. How dare you!

MERVYN. But that was what I called you last night.

(GEORGE *enters up* C)

GEORGE. She's all warmed up now, ready to go. (*He moves down* C)

(MERVYN, *who is holding Jane's hand, quickly kisses it respectfully*)

MERVYN (*very courteously*) Good-bye, Mrs Maxwell. Thank you for your wonderful hospitality. I'm sad to be leaving you. But I trust that one day I shall have the pleasure of meeting both you and your husband again. You may rest assured that I shall always remain a most devoted friend.

(MERVYN *bows stiffly to Jane and exits up* C. GEORGE *follows him to the door*)

GEORGE (*turning at the door; to Jane*) You can see the chap went to a decent school.

CURTAIN

## ACT II

### SCENE I

SCENE—*The same. Half an hour later.*

*When the* CURTAIN *rises, the divan and room have been tidied.* JANE *is telephoning.*

JANE (*into the telephone*) Oh . . . And you really think, Dr Young, that with the amount I took I could have done something without remembering? . . . Oh, heavens, yes . . . Thank you, Doctor . . . Good-bye. (*She replaces the receiver and sits on the sofa, looking perplexed*) Goodness gracious!

(*The sound of a car arriving and stopping is heard off. The voices of* GEORGE *and* MERVYN *are heard off*)

(*She rises*) Oh, no.

(GEORGE *pushes* MERVYN *into the room up* C)

GEORGE. So you've made a fool of me.

(JANE *and* MERVYN *look at each other in silence*)

Well, go on, say something.

MERVYN (*to George*) What can I say? I tried to explain in the car. But you wouldn't listen.

JANE (*to Mervyn*) You've told him everything?

MERVYN. Of course not. What do you take me for?

GEORGE. So you admit there was more.

JANE. George, it wasn't my fault. Honestly. I phoned the doctor at Dymchurch, and he said . . .

GEORGE. What has the doctor at Dymchurch got to do with it?

MERVYN. You may well ask.

GEORGE. You shut up! I'm talking to my wife. (*To Jane*) What did the doctor at Dymchurch say?

JANE. He said that after the huge dose of sleeping stuff I'd taken . . .

MERVYN. I bet he said nothing of the kind.

GEORGE. Will you kindly let my wife explain herself. Sit down.

(MERVYN *sits in the chair* C)

Well, I'm listening.

JANE. He said it's perfectly possible I wouldn't be able to remember anything that happened last night.

GEORGE. Don't start that all over again.

JANE. Phone him yourself if you don't believe me.

GEORGE. How long have I got to put up with these idiotic stories of sleeping draughts and break-downs?

JANE. I repeat, I was completely unconscious.

(MERVYN *puts up his hand and snaps his fingers like a schoolboy who wants to ask a question*)

GEORGE. Do you want to say something?

(MERVYN *nods his head*)

Well, go ahead.

MERVYN. Can I get up?

GEORGE. What for?

MERVYN. I simply can't talk when I'm sitting down. (*He rises*)

GEORGE. Right. I'm listening.

MERVYN. Well, it's this. Last night you found me in bed with your wife.

GEORGE. Do you have to stand up to say that? Sit down.

MERVYN (*losing his temper*) Can I never be allowed to finish what I'm saying? And here have I been listening to your drivel for at least an hour without getting a word in edgeways. You must think I'm a complete moron.

GEORGE (*crossing to* R) Now don't lose your temper. (*Trying to propitiate him*) You must admit that it would be a distinct advantage if we could find some explanation of the whole business.

JANE. But the doctor at Dymchurch told me . . .

GEORGE (*gently*) Jane, don't you think Mr Browne has heard enough about the doctor at Dymchurch?

MERVYN. When you've finished.

GEORGE. I was just telling my wife . . .

MERVYN. Will you stop talking? (*He speaks deliberately, slowly enunciating each syllable as if talking to a half-wit*) Mr Maxwell—I am telling you for positively the last time that my car broke down.

GEORGE. But, my dear sir, I'm perfectly willing to believe you. However, you must allow me to point out that I do find it ever so slightly odd not only that your car wasn't where you said you'd left it, but furthermore that it does seem to have vanished into thin air.

JANE. His car isn't there?

MERVYN. No. That's just the snag.

JANE (*to George*) And is that why you've been making such a fuss?

MERVYN. That's why. Can you imagine!

GEORGE. You must admit . . .

MERVYN. Will you be quiet?

JANE. Really, George, you shouldn't get me so het-up. I thought it was something far more serious.

MERVYN. Now look what you've done. You've nearly frightened poor little Mrs Maxwell out of her wits. I don't mind telling you that if I were lucky enough to be married to such a delightful wife, I wouldn't frighten her. Not on your life.

GEORGE. But really . . .

MERVYN. There's no point in you arguing. You're just a great big over-grown schoolboy.

JANE. Yes, you are.

GEORGE. Look at me, both of you.

(*They both look at him*)

Do you see anything odd?

(*They are both intrigued*)

Nothing?

JANE. No, why?

(GEORGE *turns round*)

GEORGE. As far as I can see, there's only one possible explanation. Either I'm mad or you are.

MERVYN (*with a sudden loud cry*) Tow-rope!

GEORGE. Now we know. It's him.

MERVYN. I know where she's gone to.

GEORGE. She—who?

MERVYN. You see, I phoned last night.

GEORGE. Where?

MERVYN. I've no idea.

GEORGE. What?

MERVYN (*rushing to the telephone*) They must have come and fetched her. (*He takes up the receiver. Into the telephone*) Hullo? . . . Operator? . . . Did you sleep well? . . .

JANE (*crossing to George*) He's dotty.

GEORGE. I told you so.

MERVYN (*into the telephone; facetiously*) I'm the little man with a big black beard who phoned you last night . . .

JANE (*clinging to George for protection*) You're right. We must call for help.

GEORGE. It's all right, dear. I'm here.

MERVYN (*into the telephone*) But you simply must remember. I told you my car had broken down . . . Oh, it wasn't you. (*He turns to George and Jane*) It wasn't her . . . (*Into the telephone*) Then could you please put me through to the girl with the golden voice who spoke to me so charmingly last night . . . She isn't there . . . Well, when will she be back? . . . (*To George and Jane*) She won't be back till Monday . . . (*Into the telephone*) Thank you, operator. (*He rings off*) Isn't that maddening? She isn't there, so I don't know where my car is.

GEORGE. You don't. (*He laughs*)

MERVYN. No, I don't.
GEORGE. You are a car-less chap!

(GEORGE *sees* MERVYN *looking crestfallen and bursts out laughing. His laughter is so infectious that* MERVYN *joins in. Soon both of them are doubled up with laughter*)

JANE (*crossing to the kitchen door*) I've never seen such a couple of idiots!

(JANE, *in a rage, exits to the kitchen*)

GEORGE. But joking apart, what are you going to do?
MERVYN. It really is infuriating.
GEORGE (*consulting his watch*) It's eleven twenty-five.
MERVYN. I don't see how that helps.
GEORGE. There's a bus to Dymchurch at a quarter to three. I'm not all that keen to take you. It's quite a way there and back. What would you like to do? Why don't you stay here for lunch?
MERVYN. That's out of the question.
GEORGE. Don't you want to have lunch with us?
MERVYN. I mean it's out of the question of you going all the way to Dymchurch and back.
GEORGE. But you'll stay to lunch?
MERVYN. If you're sure Mrs Maxwell won't mind.
GEORGE. I can fix that. How about a glass of sherry?
MERVYN. Excellent.
GEORGE (*crossing to the tray* R) The only problem is how to break it to her. (*He pours two glasses of sherry*)
MERVYN (*crossing to George and giving him a nudge*) Don't break anything. Just don't tell her.
GEORGE. Then she'll start breaking things.

(*They laugh*)

Do you know I can't help liking you. Whenever I look at you I want to burst out laughing. (*He hands a glass to Mervyn*)

(JANE *comes in from the kitchen, goes to the dresser and collects a dish. She wears an apron*)

MERVYN (*rolling about with laughter*) Same here! Me too!
GEORGE. Do you really?
JANE. You're right about being mad.

(GEORGE *and* MERVYN *try to control themselves*)

GEORGE. Jane, I want to tell you something. (*He hesitates and looks at Mervyn*)
JANE. Yes, what?
GEORGE (*crossing to* C) You know that Mr Browne's car has broken down . . .
JANE (*in a rage*) If you're trying to drive me mad I warn you

I shall walk out of this lounge and leave you both to stew in your own juice.

GEORGE. Juice you try! Jane, Jane, listen darling. I've asked Mr Browne . . . that's to say, I'd like to ask Mr Browne . . . (*He breaks off in embarrassment and turns to Mervyn for help. Coyly*) I mean, if you're sure you wouldn't mind if Mr Browne . . .

MERVYN (*completing the sentence*) Stayed to lunch.

GEORGE (*turning to Jane*) That's right.

JANE. There isn't enough food in the house.

(JANE *exits to the kitchen*)

GEORGE. Doesn't matter. We're not very hungry.

MERVYN. Well actually I am rather . . .

GEORGE. Oh, are you? So am I. But since my wife's being so tiresome about it, I shall go over to the farm and get some eggs.

JANE (*putting her nose round the kitchen door*) While you're about it you'd better buy a chicken. Rupert's coming down for the weekend.

GEORGE. You never told me.

JANE. We don't seem to have had much time for a gossip (*She withdraws her head*)

GEORGE. Good old Rupert! It's ages since I saw him. Righto! I'll go across to the farm. (*To Mervyn*) If any other chap turns up whose car's broken down, just chuck him out. (*He crosses and puts his glass on the tray*)

MERVYN. You can rely on me.

GEORGE. Right, shan't be long.

(GEORGE *exits up* C.

JANE *comes in from the kitchen with a tray and goes to the dresser*)

JANE. Has it occurred to you that I might not like you staying on here? (*She opens the dresser drawer*)

MERVYN. I wanted to go. But your husband was so insistent. Besides, where can I go to? The bus doesn't leave till three, and I can't bear walking.

(JANE *gets mats, cutlery and napkins from the drawer to lay the table in the garden*)

It's not only my phobia against walking. There's another reason why I want to stay.

JANE (*crossing to the door up* C) You're not going to begin that all over again, are you? (*She goes on to the terrace*)

(MERVYN *goes to the window up* LC *and watches* JANE *laying the table*)

MERVYN. I can't see why you should be offended. You ought to be flattered I'm staying on here because of you.

JANE. Well I'm not.

(MERVYN *moves and stands in front of the door up* C)

MERVYN. You don't like being told you're attractive?

JANE. I'm not really interested.

MERVYN. Good—a few moments ago it made you angry, so we're getting on fine. What's more, you're extremely intelligent.

JANE (*coldly*) Really?

MERVYN. I expect you've been told that before now.

JANE. That's why I find you so desperately boring.

MERVYN. Do you know you scare me stiff?

JANE. You look scared—I must say.

MERVYN (*moving to the window*) You should never go by appearances. When a woman really attracts me—when I feel true love—suddenly springing up in my heart like a fountain—do you know I get damn clumsy?

JANE (*coming into the room with the empty tray*) How often have you used that record?

MERVYN (*undaunted*) When I really love a woman, I want to curl up at her feet like a spaniel.

JANE (*crossing towards the kitchen door*) Do you now?

MERVYN. But most women think I'm a perfect fool.

JANE (*ironically*) Aren't women funny?

(JANE *exits to the kitchen*)

MERVYN (*crossing to the kitchen door*) Women fall for the more active type. You know—strong, muscular, a bit rough at times. Women fall for men who are utter brutes.

JANE (*off*) Not all women do.

MERVYN. Don't they? My trouble is I'm too sensitive. I was a delicate child.

(JANE *enters from the kitchen. She carries a basket of cut bread and a bowl of fruit on the tray*)

JANE. You were right when you said one should never go by appearances.

MERVYN (*cornering her by the door*) But there's one thing I do regret.

JANE. What?

MERVYN. I'm terribly sorry about last night.

JANE (*evading him*) You may well be. (*She collects the cruet from the dresser*)

MERVYN. Don't misunderstand me. I've never known a more wonderful evening in all my life.

JANE. Really! (*She goes out to the garden in a rage*)

MERVYN (*following her to the door*) I only wish we could have got to know each other better.

JANE. Better? (*She puts the bread, fruit and cruet on the table*)

MERVYN. More gradually. I'd have liked to have been introduced to you, then I'd have got to know you, then I'd have begun to . . .
JANE (*putting her head through the window*) Curl up at my feet?
MERVYN. Precisely. Then to tell you how beautiful you are. Then I'd have a few moments of hope—then of despair. Then I'd suffer anguish because of you.
JANE (*coming in to the room with the empty tray*) For how long?
MERVYN. Well not all that long. But gradually, bit by bit, I'd win you over . . . Until finally, you'd be only too glad—if you get my meaning.
JANE. Only too well. (*She crosses to the kitchen door*) So don't let's discuss it any more. You can catch the three-o'clock bus after lunch and get into the back of your car and curl up there. Like a spaniel.

(JANE *exits to the kitchen.* MERVYN *moves below the sofa*)

MERVYN (*trying to sound wretched*) You're very unkind to me.
JANE (*off*) You're very good at putting on an act.
MERVYN. What! You don't think I'm genuine?

(JANE *enters from the kitchen*)

JANE. I'm certain you're not.
MERVYN. Do you think I'm a heartless brute? Do you think that what happened last night could have taken place if I hadn't . . .

(JANE *makes a gesture of protest*)

No, I must speak—even if it does upset you. Can't you see that it wasn't our fault? Circumstances were just too strong for us. I won't speak of fate or you'll think I'm putting on an act again. But I'm certain that's what happened and I shall never forget it. Why, I can remember every detail. And you think I've never known what it is to love.
JANE (*crossing to* C) You say you'll never forget it?
MERVYN. Never.
JANE. And you remember it all clearly?
MERVYN. I can give you every single detail.
JANE (*sitting in the chair* C) Good. Let's have them.
MERVYN (*astonished*) What?
JANE. I want you to give me the details.
MERVYN (*still taken aback*) You want me to?
JANE. Yes.
MERVYN. Oh, I simply couldn't. We scarcely know each other.
JANE. Even after those two glorious hours before my husband came in?
MERVYN. So it's all come back to you?
JANE. Nothing's come back to me. That's why I want proof.

MERVYN. But how can I give you proof?
JANE. Quite easily—if what you've said is true. Just tell me what happened last night.
MERVYN. You'd like me to tell you?
JANE. Yes.
MERVYN. Very well. It's quite simple. I arrived here. I knocked on the door but no-one answered, so I walked in and found you asleep. I was tip-toeing away, when you woke up. I asked if I could ring up a garage. You said I could. So I did. Then I went over to thank you. And you were perfectly enchanting. You smiled up at me. And I smiled back.
JANE. So we smiled at each other.
MERVYN. That's right. Well, then I held your hand—and you held mine. And you looked up at me with those wonderful eyes of yours—your hands were quite hot. Mine were stone cold—and you said—you said: "What cold hands you have." And I said—I said: "Yes, but I've a warm heart."
JANE. That was very witty.
MERVYN. No. It wasn't. I didn't know what to say—I was extremely moved—I could feel my heart pounding away like a mad thing.
JANE. And then?

(MERVYN *is confused. He does not know quite what to say next*)

MERVYN. Right. Well, we talked for a bit. Then you ran your fingers lightly through my hair and you said: "Where did you spring from, handsome stranger?"
JANE. I said that, did I?
MERVYN. Those were your very words.
JANE. The light must have been very bad. And then what happened?
MERVYN (*who is getting more and more put off by Jane's sarcasm*) Well then I took you in my arms—like so. (*He tries to embrace her*)
JANE. Never mind the acting. Just relax and give me the plain facts.
MERVYN. How can I possibly relax?
JANE. Up to now I've still had no proof . . .
MERVYN. What more proof do you want, for heaven's sake?
JANE. Carry on and we'll see.
MERVYN. If you insist. But stop me if you feel like it. Now, where had we got to?
JANE (*very calmly*) You were holding me in your arms.
MERVYN. Yes. Well, then I had one of the biggest shocks of my life.
JANE. Really?
MERVYN. Up to that moment you'd been quite placid. Suddenly you changed. Oh, you were terrific! You twined yourself round me. Our lips met in a burning kiss. I could feel the softness

of your skin against mine. (*He is beginning to get carried away by his own enthusiasm*)

(JANE *still listens imperturbably*)

You just weren't the same person. Your whole being trembled in my embrace. You clutched me in a frenzy. By the light of the hunter's moon softly filtering through the trees I could see the shadows of the leaves gently swaying over your breast. Oh, you were tremendous!

JANE. And then?

MERVYN. Well then—you held my hand.

JANE. Was it still stone cold?

MERVYN. No, it was beginning to warm up, and you said: "Angel one, look at me". When you called me "Angel one", my passion got too strong for me. I just couldn't control myself an instant longer.

JANE. And then?

MERVYN. I wonder if I could trouble you for a glass of water?

JANE. Presently.

MERVYN. You're not a bit sympathetic. Can't you see that living through the whole thing again has given me a raging thirst?

JANE. You shouldn't get so over-excited. Finish your story.

MERVYN. You really want the details?

JANE. Every single one of them.

MERVYN. Right up to the very end?

JANE. To the very end.

MERVYN. Your interest is positively indecent.

JANE. I need to know various points to find out if you're telling the truth or not.

MERVYN. You want me to go on?

JANE. Please do.

MERVYN (*inspired*) We fell into each other's arms again. I could feel your nails digging into my neck.

JANE. Have you still got the marks?

MERVYN. No, you only dug very gently.

JANE. Pity. You might have had some proof at last—however, carry on.

MERVYN. Then you said . . .

JANE. You're still using my very words?

MERVYN. Certainly. You said: "Not yet, not yet."

JANE. You make me tired.

MERVYN. I certainly did. You were completely exhausted. But I said: "Jane, my darling."

JANE. You knew my name?

MERVYN. We'd introduced ourselves a few minutes previously.

JANE. I see.

MERVYN. Then for two hours it was absolute heaven. Finally, you went to sleep on my shoulder.

JANE (*rising in a rage*) Stop it!

MERVYN. But you asked me to tell you.

JANE. I wanted to see how far you would go with your disgusting lies. There's not one word of truth in all you've said.

MERVYN. You don't believe me?

JANE. I wanted proof. I've got it. I now know you've been lying all the time.

MERVYN. How can you be so sure when you admit you can't remember what happened?

JANE. There's one thing you didn't mention—something you couldn't possibly have forgotten.

MERVYN. Something I wouldn't have forgotten? Whatever can that be?

JANE (*crossing angrily towards the kitchen door*) Something . . . Forget it.

MERVYN. You interest me strangely. Wait. Let me think. You've got some kind of—peculiarity?

JANE (*angrier than ever*) One more word out of you and I'll smack your face.

(GEORGE *enters up* C, *with a shopping basket*)

GEORGE. Hullo. Have you two made it up?

(JANE *stalks out to the kitchen without answering*)

(*He stares after Jane in astonishment*) Oh, dear! Still no go?

MERVYN. I think she'll end up by liking me.

GEORGE (*deliberately changing the subject*) Do you mind if I put through a call to London? We've got a big deal on, the office may have news for me. You don't mind? (*He puts the basket on the table up* LC)

MERVYN. Of course not. May I have a glass of water?

GEORGE. Of course, my dear fellow, help yourself.

MERVYN. Don't think I'm being inquisitive, but what's your line? (*He goes to the tray* R *and pours a glass of water*)

GEORGE. Oil.

MERVYN. Olive oil? (*He drinks and replaces the glass*)

GEORGE. No. Lubricating.

MERVYN. Now, isn't that fantastic!

GEORGE. Why? (*He moves down* C)

MERVYN. Well, because I happen to be the Commercial Manager of North American Oils Incorporated.

GEORGE (*most impressed*) Really! Isn't that just amazing! Do you know that I happen to be specializing in reconditioned oils at this very moment? I promise you that we've reached a point where we can recondition a reclaimed oil with absolutely perfect results. Here you have an oil which has all the virtues of a virgin

oil—with the enormous advantage of selling at a much lower price. It works out at a difference of between twopence-halfpenny and threepence a gallon—that's as delivered straight from the factory, of course.
MERVYN. Of course, I see that.
GEORGE (*beside himself with excitement*) Let's talk about it over lunch. Fancy you being Commercial Manager of N.A.O.I. Would you believe it! You know, I'd very much like to have some kind of tie-up with your firm. Listen, I've just thought of something. Did you say your car wouldn't be ready till Monday?
MERVYN. Yes.
GEORGE. Then you must stay over Sunday with us.
MERVYN (*pretending to protest*) Really, I couldn't. You've been so wonderfully hospitable as it is.
GEORGE. But I should be delighted if you could stay.
MERVYN. You're sure I'm not being a nuisance?
GEORGE. Not in the least! So you will stay, won't you?
MERVYN. What will Mrs Maxwell say?
GEORGE. She won't say anything—just you see. (*He calls*) Jane! Not that it matters if she does object. (*He calls*) Jane!

(JANE *enters from the kitchen*)

JANE. You called me?
GEORGE. I've just asked Mr Browne to stay with us over the weekend.

(JANE *goes out without replying and slams the door behind her*)

MERVYN. Well—she didn't say no.

*The lights* BLACK-OUT *as—*

*the* CURTAIN *falls*

SCENE 2

SCENE—*The same. After lunch that day.*
*When the* CURTAIN *rises,* GEORGE *is holding forth on the benefits of reconditioned oils with the assistance of coloured lantern slides. There is a projector on the stool* C, *focused on a screen up* C. *There is a complicated-looking graph on the screen. The window curtains are closed and the light is dim.* JANE *and* MERVYN *are bored stiff. They are holding coffee cups and saucers.* JANE *is seated on the sofa.* MERVYN *is seated on the rocking chair which is now down* R.

GEORGE. Now, on examining the chart closely the first thing we observe is the rapid rise in production of reconditioned oils since nineteen forty-two. In that year alone we produced three thousand tons of engine oils—which rose as high as twenty-five thousand tons in nineteen fifty-six.

(MERVYN *rises and crosses to Jane*)

MERVYN. May I take your cup, Mrs Maxwell?
JANE. Oh, thank you. (*She hands her cup to Mervyn*)

(MERVYN *crosses in front of the screen and stands up* R)

GEORGE. Hmm—excuse me, old man. Now let's take Industrial Oils. (*He inserts a new and yet more complicated graph*) In nineteen fifty-two, the production of Industrial Oils was practically nil, yet it's over ten thousand tons today. And why?
MERVYN. I don't really know.
GEORGE (*putting in a new slide of a factory*) I'll show you. Because the great mistake is to think of a reconditioned oil as being simply a filtered oil. That's what I want to impress on you. You've only to look at our installations to see that the oils we reclaim undergo a positive refining process.

(JANE *giggles*)

The impure . . .
MERVYN (*to Jane*) What are you laughing at?
JANE. It's you with those coffee cups. (*She rises*)
GEORGE. The impure oil . . .

(MERVYN *crosses to Jane and gives her the cups*)

JANE. I'll put them in the kitchen—sorry.

(JANE *exits to the kitchen.* GEORGE *puts in a new slide of a refinery. Each time he turns his back to find a new slide,* MERVYN *puts his hand in front of the lantern and makes funny shadows on the screen.* JANE *re-enters and sits on the sofa*)

GEORGE. The impure oils are entirely regenerated. Now just to show you the difference between a filtered oil and a regenerated oil. (*He puts in a slide of a test-tube with dirty green oil in it*) There you see the colour of oil that has only been filtered. Now this is the colour of a regenerated oil. (*He inserts a new slide, a test tube containing a yellow oil*) There you see that beautiful clear yellow tint you know so well. And I can assure you that not one single drop of oil leaves our factories without being thoroughly tested in our laboratories. (*He puts in another slide, a chemist in his laboratory*) And I can furthermore guarantee that . . .
JANE. You're a crashing bore!
GEORGE. I beg your pardon.
JANE. I can furthermore guarantee that you're a crashing bore.
GEORGE. If I'm boring you, darling, why don't you go out into the garden?
JANE. I'd already thought of that.
GEORGE. Mr Browne happens to be extremely interested. Aren't you, Mr Browne?

MERVYN (*trying to sound enthusiastic*) Extremely. (*He crosses to the chair down* R) But as you know I already understand the basic problem, so ... (*He sits*)

GEORGE. I could have cut out my preamble. Now the whole point is this ...

JANE. George, before I go into the garden, I want a word with you.

GEORGE (*to Mervyn*) There's no chance of any serious conversation while she's around.

MERVYN. We must remember it's rather a sticky subject for a young lady. Couldn't we talk about dress designing?

JANE. Don't bother. Just a word with my husband and I'll leave you both to it.

GEORGE (*who is longing to get back to his discussion*) All right. Quickly now. What is it?

JANE. Rupert arrives this evening.

GEORGE. I know. So what?

JANE. Where's he going to sleep?

GEORGE. In the room above the garage. Where d'you think?

JANE. And I suppose you'll put Mr Browne on our divan?

MERVYN. Please don't let me inconvenience you.

GEORGE. I hadn't thought of that. Well, they'll just both have to double up. After all, it's only for two nights. (*To Mervyn*) You won't mind, will you?

MERVYN (*unenthusiastically*) Of course not, my dear fellow.

GEORGE. I bet you served in the Forces.

MERVYN (*with a shudder*) I did.

GEORGE. Then you certainly won't mind roughing it.

MERVYN. No, but—er ...

JANE. Perhaps you'd rather I slept over the garage with Rupert and you slept here with Mr Browne? Then you could talk oil all night long.

GEORGE (*to Mervyn*) When my wife makes a joke it's almost always in bad taste.

JANE. I haven't your purity of soul, George.

GEORGE. I'm sure you haven't, my dear. Now, will you please leave us alone?

(JANE *rises and exits up* C)

Where had I got to? Oh, yes, I know. Now to return to where I left off ...

MERVYN (*trying to cut him short*) Oughtn't we to do something about Mrs Maxwell?

GEORGE. She's never interested when I talk business.

MERVYN. Couldn't we talk about something else? When I'm in the country, I make it a rule never to talk shop.

GEORGE. Oh, very well. (*He looks most annoyed*)

MERVYN. I'm not blaming you, my dear fellow. I'm only

pointing out that we spend the whole week shut up in our offices, so we deserve a good rest over the weekend.

GEORGE. You're perfectly right. I'm afraid I've been boring you. (*He switches off the projector*)

MERVYN. But on the contrary! I'm absolutely fascinated.

(*This gives* GEORGE *new hope. He switches on the projector again*)

(*He rises*) What's more, we must meet in London and discuss the whole matter at length. But when I'm in the country I like breathing the fresh air. (*He draws back the curtains*) I like wandering across the fields gathering wild flowers—without so much as a thought in my head.

GEORGE (*packing up the projector*) I wish I could do that, but my head's always buzzing with ideas. (*He packs up the screen*)

MERVYN. You make a great mistake. (*He looks at the tray* R) That looks exactly like a bottle of Chartreuse over there. I know you'll think me a monstrous old soak.

GEORGE. But of course, my dear chap. Forgive me for not thinking of it before—though it's really your hostess's job. Not that there's much hope in that direction. (*He crosses to the tray* R)

MERVYN. Don't be too hard on her.

(MERVYN *holds a glass up for* GEORGE *to fill*)

GEORGE. Look! That's it!

MERVYN. What?

GEORGE. The very colour of reconditioned oil.

MERVYN. You trying to put me off?

GEORGE. Oh, I'm so sorry.

MERVYN. Are you going to have one?

GEORGE. Not at the moment. Were you at the Eighth International Congress on Lubricators and their Derivatives last March?

MERVYN. No, I was too busy at the time. I was most disappointed. Tell me—this Rupert Shaughnessy who's coming down . . .

GEORGE. Rupert Shaughnessy?

MERVYN. Yes. The chap you spoke about just now.

GEORGE. His name isn't Shaughnessy.

MERVYN. Isn't it?

GEORGE. No, it's Arkwright.

MERVYN. Arkwright! He's not a chap with fair hair?

GEORGE. No. His hair's brown.

MERVYN. When I say fair, I mean his hair's not absolutely black. I mean I wouldn't describe him as a Spanish type.

GEORGE. Certainly not.

MERVYN. His hair's more a kind of chestnut . . .

GEORGE. Yes, I suppose it is.

MERVYN. That's it.
GEORGE. With a small moustache.
MERVYN. With a small light brown moustache. About so high.

(MERVYN *raises his hand slowly, hoping that* GEORGE *will stop him when he has reached the right height.* MERVYN *has reached the height of a giant when* GEORGE *speaks*)

GEORGE. He's not very tall.

(MERVYN *hastily lowers his hand*)

MERVYN. In fact I'd say he was rather on the short side. Wouldn't you?
GEORGE. Yes, I think I would.
MERVYN. And he works in some . . .
GEORGE. Some firm that makes plastics.
MERVYN. That's him right enough. Isn't that amazing?
GEORGE. You know him?
MERVYN. Do I know him? I'll say I know him!
GEORGE. Good heavens! (*He calls*) Jane! Jane! Isn't the world a small place?
MERVYN. Absolutely tiny.
GEORGE (*calling*) Jane! Just heard some astounding news.

(JANE *appears at the door up* C)

Mr Browne knows Rupert Arkwright.
MERVYN. I certainly do. He's not very tall with light brown hair and a small moustache and he works in some branch of plastics.

(JANE *looks at George in amazement*)

Until quite recently he'd got a girl-friend—a married woman. I've never met her. But I gather she was nothing to write home about.
GEORGE. Fancy old Rupert having a girl-friend! (*To Jane*) Did you know that?
MERVYN. He certainly had. But it's all washed up now. For the past few weeks he's been going round with a young artist's model.

(JANE *winces*)

Oh, what an attractive creature! I can't make her out. Because between you and me, Rupert's got a face like the back of a cab.
GEORGE (*laughing*) Yes, but not so handsome!

(JANE *stalks out up* C)

MERVYN (*crossing and looking out of the window up* LC; *pretending to be surprised*) Now what have I said to annoy her?

GEORGE. I can't imagine.

MERVYN. Perhaps I shocked her when I said that old Rupert had a girl-friend?

GEORGE. Jane's no prude.

MERVYN. All the same, I'm terribly sorry.

GEORGE. My dear fellow, doesn't matter a scrap.

MERVYN. But there's one thing that does worry me.

GEORGE. Forget it.

MERVYN. I can't quite. You see, it's about Rupert.

GEORGE. Tell me.

MERVYN. Perhaps I'd better not.

GEORGE. Why?

MERVYN. Well, if he comes I'll have to go. It's just something personal between him and me.

GEORGE. What?

MERVYN. I'm afraid he's a bad type.

GEORGE. Bad type? He can't be. I was at school with him.

MERVYN. I don't want to say anything against a friend of yours. But so far as I'm concerned I hope I never set eyes on him again.

GEORGE. What's he been up to?

MERVYN. Well, I'd advise you not to invite him here too often, he's the kind of man who'll think nothing of having an affair with the wife of his best friend.

GEORGE. Rupert is? (*He crosses to* C)

MERVYN. And that's not all. But I can't tell you the rest.

GEORGE. You can't?

MERVYN. I simply couldn't.

GEORGE. I'm amazed.

MERVYN. Now perhaps you understand why I couldn't possibly share the same room with the chap.

GEORGE. I certainly do.

MERVYN. Would you think me very rude if I took another tiny little drink? (*He crosses to* R)

GEORGE. Help yourself.

MERVYN (*pouring a drink for himself*) Thanks. I'm sorry that because of Rupert I shall now have to leave you today. I'll be away from London for the next two or three weeks. I'd so much have liked another chat—tomorrow—about your degenerated oil.

GEORGE. You mean regenerated.

MERVYN. Of course I do. When I said degenerated I was still thinking of Rupert. I'm sure it's a matter which would interest our Administrative Council. And as you know we deal in vast consignments. However, it'll just have to wait till I get back.

GEORGE. When should we meet?

MERVYN. Well, that's the trouble. You see, when I get back, I'll have to leave almost immediately for Holland, and I don't know how long I shall have to stay there.

GEORGE. That's really bad luck, but I do see that with things as they are you can't possibly share a bed with the man.
MERVYN. I wouldn't even sit at the same table. No, we'll just have to wait three months. It's a pity though. We might have had quite a long talk tomorrow.
GEORGE. Supposing I phoned and put Rupert off?
MERVYN. Oh, you couldn't do that.
GEORGE. Why not?
MERVYN. You'd have to be very tactful.
GEORGE. I could tell him I didn't know he was coming so I'd already invited someone else.
MERVYN. Then for heaven's sake don't tell him it's me.
GEORGE. Of course not. (*He hesitates*)
MERVYN. Why not phone him right away? (*He crosses to the telephone*) It would be sad if he came all this way down here for nothing. (*He lifts the receiver and holds it out to George*)
GEORGE (*taking the receiver; very embarrassed*) You're perfectly right. (*Into the telephone*) Hullo? . . . Exchange? . . . Can you give me London—Flaxman one-three-seven-five. (*To Mervyn*) I'm amazed. The wives of his very best friends?
MERVYN. He's an absolute swine.
GEORGE (*into the telephone*) Hullo? . . . Yes, I'm still holding on . . .
MERVYN. If I were you I wouldn't tell your wife you put him off because of what I said. You never know. It might turn her against me.
GEORGE. I shall tell her that he rang up and called it off.
MERVYN. Brilliant idea. I should never have thought of it.
GEORGE (*into the telephone*) Hullo? . . . Rupert? . . . George here . . . How are you? I haven't seen you for ages . . . Yes, I mean, no . . . (*He is thoroughly embarrassed*) That's just what I'm phoning about. Something most tiresome has happened. (*He glances at Mervyn for approval*) You see, I didn't know you were coming down—Jane's only just told me . . . Yes, she's very well, thank you . . .
MERVYN (*aside*) The swine!
GEORGE (*to Mervyn*) What?

(MERVYN *puts his fingers to his lips*)

(*into the telephone*) And just guess what's happened this end . . . Since I didn't know you were coming, I've asked someone else for the weekend . . . Put him off? (*He looks to Mervyn for help*)

(MERVYN *shakes his head*)

No, I'm afraid I can't. He's a very old friend of mine.

(MERVYN *does a military salute*)

We were in the same regiment . . . Can't be helped? What do

you mean? . . . Oh, I see! Can't be helped and you won't come. That's splendid . . . No, no. I mean, I'm very sorry, but we'll have to leave it for another . . . Hullo? . . . Hullo, Rupert? (*He turns to Mervyn*) Would you believe it? He's hung up on me.

MERVYN. Typical of the cad. What about a quick snort?

GEORGE (*replacing the receiver*) Yes—so you're going off on a business trip?

MERVYN. Am I? (*He crosses to* R, *pours a drink for George and refills his own glass*)

GEORGE. Yes. (*He crosses to Mervyn*)

MERVYN. Oh, definitely! Yes, I am. I'm leaving . . . Of course, it's not *absolutely* certain yet when.

GEORGE. I'd like to explain the entire project to you.

MERVYN (*handing him a glass*) We can talk business tomorrow.

(JANE *enters up* C, *carrying a marrow*)

GEORGE (*taking the glass*) Thanks. Perhaps I ought to break the news to her.

MERVYN. Why not do it right away?

(JANE *crosses towards the kitchen door*)

GEORGE. A good idea. Jane!
JANE (*stopping and turning*) Yes?
GEORGE. Jane, I've got something to tell you.
JANE. What?
GEORGE. Oh, yes—Rupert has just phoned up.
JANE (*eagerly*) What did he say?
GEORGE. He rang up to say that—that he wouldn't be able to come down this weekend.
MERVYN. I expect something cropped up at the last moment. In that Plastic business you never know what'll happen next.

(JANE *exits to the kitchen*)

GEORGE. What in heaven's name's the matter with her today?
MERVYN. She seems a bit on edge. It's probably this heat wave.
GEORGE. My dear man, how I envy you?
MERVYN. Why?
GEORGE. Being a bachelor.
MERVYN. Oh, well, it has definite advantages, you know. There's a glorious sense of freedom. One can go after any girl one likes. There's the excitement of finding out how each girl's different from the rest. Her own particular little ways.
GEORGE. Quite.
MERVYN. When you were young I bet you had a rare old time?
GEORGE (*modestly*) Oh, I wouldn't say that.
MERVYN. You must have had some tremendous adventures?

GEORGE. As a matter of fact I did. I was on safari in Tanganyika once, and I actually shot a crocodile.
MERVYN (*not at all interested*) Did you now?
GEORGE. I was twenty-seven at the time. And there was this huge crocodile...
MERVYN. You must tell me the whole story when we meet in London. But to return to our most interesting discussion—women are full of surprises. You meet a girl, you think she's going to be the same as all the rest. Then, suddenly she turns out to be entirely different.
GEORGE. You don't say?
MERVYN. In your time you must have found some completely unexpected trait in a girl—some unusual peculiarity you just couldn't forget?
GEORGE (*trying to remember*) I don't think so.
MERVYN. You never came across anything out of the ordinary — anything a bit odd?
GEORGE. I can't say I have.
MERVYN. You never came across any particular idiosyncrasy, mannerism or quirk?

(GEORGE *thinks for a moment, then bursts out laughing*)

GEORGE. Yes, I have, now I come to think of it. When I was a subaltern—it must have been in 'forty. No, it wasn't. It was 'forty-one—I must have been about twenty-two—twenty-three at the most. It was about three years before I met Jane. No, I'm wrong—it was four. Anyhow I met this girl on leave. She was a bit older than I was but she had a smashing figure. Well, do you know what her little peculiarity was?
MERVYN. No.
GEORGE (*laughing so much at the thought of it he can hardly speak; he imitates a Chinese lisp*) Shle shploke shlike shlat.
MERVYN (*most disappointed*) Did she really?

(MERVYN *turns to go out by the door up* C. GEORGE *follows him, determined to finish his story*)

GEORGE. When she phoned me she used to say: "Is shlat Shloane shleven shlix shlix shleven?" (*He roars with laughter*)

(MERVYN *is not amused*)

But apart from that she was quite a pet. She married an Air Vice-Marshal with a stammer.
MERVYN (*despondently*) But didn't you ever meet a girl with some more bizarre trait—something a bit more intimate?
GEORGE. But you see after that I got married.
MERVYN. Quite.
GEORGE. Since that day I've given other wenches a miss.

MERVYN (*sighing and moving to the bookcase* R) Hot today, isn't it?

GEORGE. Do you know this time last year it was raining in torrents?

MERVYN. Was it really? I wonder if I could possibly borrow a book? I feel I need a rest.

GEORGE (*crossing to the bookcase* R) I know the very one.

MERVYN. I quite like thrillers if you've got any.

GEORGE (*handing him a book*) You'll find this more exciting than any thriller.

(MERVYN *reads the title through his teeth*)

MERVYN. "*Lubricants and their Derivatives.*"

GEORGE. There's a remarkable chapter on "Reconditioned Oil".

MERVYN. I bet it's positively gripping.

GEORGE. You read that and tell me what you think of it. (*He crosses and sits on the sofa*)

(MERVYN *sits down* R *and pretends to read*)

(*He watches Mervyn for a few moments, then smiles*) I say—I've just thought of something.

MERVYN (*bored*) What?

GEORGE. About girls who are peculiar.

MERVYN (*suddenly interested*) Yes? Do tell me.

GEORGE (*rising*) I don't know if I should . . .

MERVYN (*rising and crossing to George*) Please.

GEORGE. No, I really can't. It's silly—but it just amuses me.

MERVYN. I'm sure it'll amuse me too.

GEORGE. Well, when I got to know—shall we say a certain person . . .

MERVYN. Yes?

GEORGE (*with a little bashful laugh*) I really don't know why I'm telling you this. Well then . . .

MERVYN (*eagerly*) Yes. I get you. Carry on.

GEORGE. This certain person never talks.

MERVYN. No?

GEORGE. She just says the same two words over and over again.

MERVYN. Yes?

GEORGE. Don't you think that's funny?

MERVYN. What two words?

GEORGE. "No. Please."

MERVYN. Don't be modest.

GEORGE. But I've just told you.

MERVYN. What?

GEORGE. The two words.

MERVYN. You certainly have not.

GEORGE. Yes I have. "No. Please."

MERVYN. She says, "No. Please"?
GEORGE. Yes.
MERVYN. Evidently she doesn't know her own mind.
GEORGE. Oh, I wouldn't say that.
MERVYN (*curtly*) Do forgive me, but I must finish this chapter. (*He sits on the sofa*)

(GEORGE *looks at him in amazement.* MERVYN *takes up his book and pretends to be engrossed in it*)

GEORGE. I hope you find it as exciting as I did. I couldn't put it down. (*He sits beside Mervyn on the sofa*)
MERVYN. Going out for a walk?
GEORGE. I don't want to leave you all on your own.
MERVYN. Please don't bother about me.
GEORGE. As a matter of fact, I'm not all that keen on walking. But I have to find something to do. So I go and call on the neighbours. They're quite a decent lot. And we've a first-class shoot.
MERVYN. Why don't you go out shooting today?
GEORGE. In July?
MERVYN. I wasn't thinking. What's the fishing like round here?
GEORGE. Rotten. There's no stream.
MERVYN (*getting exasperated*) Well what *are* you going to do all day?
GEORGE. Well, if you wouldn't honestly mind and didn't think I was a rotten host, I really would like to leave you for an hour.
MERVYN. My dear fellow, when you get to know me you'll realize I wouldn't mind if you left me alone for all of *two* hours. I swear I wouldn't mind a scrap.
GEORGE. Thanks awfully. (*He rises*) Then I think I'll go and see old Briggs—our carpenter—about that garage door he ought to have mended.
MERVYN. That's right. And don't give me a thought. This book will last me at least three hours.
GEORGE. Help yourself to another drink if you want it. I won't be long.
MERVYN. Don't hurry.

(GEORGE *exits up* C.

JANE, *looking depressed, enters from the kitchen. She crosses to* R *and looks out at the garden.* MERVYN *pretends to be reading*)

Delightful weather, isn't it?
JANE. Yes. (*She pours a drink for herself*)

(*There is a pause*)

MERVYN. Do you know this time last year it was raining in torrents.
JANE. Yes.

MERVYN (*putting down his book*) Does my conversation bore you? (*He rises*)
JANE. Yes.
MERVYN (*moving to her*) You don't want to talk to me?
JANE. No.
MERVYN. Please don't think of me as an enemy. I do so want us to be friends.

(JANE *does not reply. She is deep in thought*)

Do you still hate me?
JANE (*moving to the sofa*) I'm completely indifferent to you. (*She sits on the sofa*)
MERVYN. That's even worse.

(JANE *picks up the book and puts it down*)

MERVYN (*moving to Jane; very gently*) I'm sure you're unhappy about something. I do wish I could help.
JANE. There's nothing you can do.
MERVYN. How do you know?
JANE (*rising*) Please leave me alone.
MERVYN. All I ask is let's be friends. (*He holds out his hand*)

(*After a moment's hesitation,* JANE *holds out hers and they shake hands*)

Do you know I suspect you take life far too seriously.
JANE. Why do you say that? (*She sits on the sofa*)
MERVYN. Because I can see you're unhappy, and I wonder if life is really that serious. Now we're friends you won't mind if I tell you that you're very lovely. You're in perfect health. You don't need to worry about money. What more do you want?
JANE (*thoughtfully*) I suppose you're right. (*She drinks*)
MERVYN. Most people would envy you.
JANE. Perhaps so.
MERVYN. Life's got such wonderful things in store for you. Now smile.

(JANE *smiles faintly*)

You can do better than that. Come on now. Give me a great big smile.

(JANE *gives a little laugh*)

That's better! You've either been sad or in a rage all morning. This is the very first time you've smiled.
JANE. You know, I think you're a clown.
MERVYN. A clown?
JANE. Yes, but a nice one.
MERVYN. I'm glad we're friends. You must have a pretty low opinion of me. I'm ashamed of myself.

JANE. Please don't let's talk about it.
MERVYN. Then will you forget everything I said.
JANE. It's all forgotten. (*She drinks*) Let's say I had amnesia.
MERVYN. Damnesia said than done.
JANE (*groaning at the pun*) You're worse than George.

(*They both laugh.* MERVYN *settles down on the floor beside her*)

(*She laughs*) Are you starting to curl up?
MERVYN. What do you mean?
JANE. Don't say you've forgotten how you always curl up at ladies' feet?
MERVYN (*looking sad*) Now you're laughing at me. You won't take me seriously.
JANE. Why should I? And you don't give a hoot.
MERVYN. Now you've really hurt me.
JANE (*vaguely*) I can't see why.
MERVYN. You must think I'm an utter fraud.
JANE. Let's say a slight fraud.
MERVYN. Do you really imagine I haven't got it?
JANE. Haven't got what?
MERVYN. The proof you wanted.
JANE. Then let's have it.
MERVYN. No, please.
JANE. Well?
MERVYN (*slowly*) No, please.

(JANE *begins to understand*)

(*Quicker*) No. Please. No. Please. No. Please.

(JANE *springs to her feet*)

(*He rises and catches hold of her*) Jane!
JANE (*struggling*) Let me go!

(MERVYN *forces Jane down on to the sofa*)

MERVYN. Jane, forgive me.
JANE. Be quiet! (*She sits on the sofa*)
MERVYN. Jane—my little darling. (*He kisses her hands*)

(JANE *puts her hand over his mouth*)

JANE. No. Please. (*She stares at Mervyn, then starts to kiss him*)

(GEORGE *enters up* C)

GEORGE. Old Briggs wasn't in, worse luck.

(MERVYN *drops Jane's hands like hot bricks and begins to crawl on all fours as if searching for something*)

MERVYN. Where did you think you dropped it?

CURTAIN

## ACT III

SCENE—*The same. The same evening.*

*When the* CURTAIN *rises, the lights are on and the music of "Mr Wonderful" is coming from the radio.* JANE *is lying on the sofa.* MERVYN *is standing down* L. GEORGE *is hunting for something in a large metal tool-box on the dresser, and making a lot of noise about it. After a few moments,* GEORGE, *grumbling to himself, exits to the kitchen.* MERVYN *crosses to the sofa, takes Jane's hand and tries to kiss her.*

MERVYN. Jane!
JANE. Careful! He might see us.
MERVYN. I've so much to say to you.
JANE. Then say it from a safe distance.

(MERVYN *moves to the rocking chair* C)

MERVYN. Jane, what I wanted to say . . .

(*The sound of hammering is heard off* L)

(*He raises his voice*) I've known better occasions for a talk. (*He sits*) Jane, this is what I was trying to say—you're going to be furious with me but I can't help it—Jane—I believe I'm really in love with you.
JANE. What's that?

(*The sound of hammering ceases*)

MERVYN. I believe I'm really in love with you.

(GEORGE *appears in the kitchen doorway*)

GEORGE (*to Jane*) Have you taken my hammer?
JANE. Why should I want your old hammer?
GEORGE (*crossly*) Really, it's infuriating . . .
JANE. You'll find it on the shelf above your bench.
GEORGE (*still angrier*) I don't mean the big hammer. I mean the little one.
JANE (*also crossly*) So do I mean the little one. Follow your own nose and you'll find it.
GEORGE (*as he goes out muttering*) It's just maddening; I can never keep a thing of my own in this house. I suppose the damn painters had it upstairs.

(GEORGE *exits to the kitchen and shuts the door*)

JANE (*rising*) He simply drives me dotty.

(MERVYN *rises, moves to Jane, takes her hands and calms her*)

MERVYN. Let's forget about him.

(JANE *stares at him for an instant in silence*)

JANE. How strange it is looking at you and thinking about last night.

MERVYN. I suppose it must seem a bit odd.

(JANE *puts her arms round his neck*)

JANE. Say something nice to me. I do so want to be made a fuss of.

MERVYN. Jane, there's something I must tell you.

JANE (*running her fingers through his hair*) Where did you spring from, handsome stranger?

MERVYN. Well, you see, my car broke down.

JANE (*moving away from him and laughing*) Not that one! Tell me more about the moonlight.

MERVYN. Quite. Well now. To be honest with you—actually, I did exaggerate just a little. The shadow of the leaves, for instance, wasn't a hundred per cent accurate.

JANE. Wasn't there any moon?

MERVYN. Yes. But it didn't make any shadows on your breast.

(GEORGE *starts singing off*)

JANE. No? (*Slowly*) What about the rest of your story?

MERVYN. As to the rest of it . . .

(GEORGE *enters from the kitchen.* JANE *sits on the sofa.* MERVYN *moves quickly to the radio and turns it off.* GEORGE *takes no notice of them. He rummages noisily in the dresser drawer grumbling under his breath. Suddenly he pulls out a pound of sausages from the drawer and flourishes it under* JANE'S *nose*)

GEORGE. And what may I ask is this?

JANE. Oh, good, I knew those sausages would turn up sooner or later.

GEORGE (*pointing to the drawer*) Is that the proper place for sausages? Sausages should be wrapped in aluminium foil and put in the refrigerator.

JANE. Then why don't you put them there? (*She rises, snatches the sausages away from him and puts them in the tool-box*)

GEORGE. Well, it's really hardly my job.

JANE. A maid of all work. That's all I am. (*She slams down the lid of the box, lifts the box with an effort, and thrusts it into George's hands*)

GEORGE (*holding the box*) Mr Browne, I really must apologize.

MERVYN. Don't mind me.

GEORGE. But I do mind you. And I find it perfectly disgraceful. When a man's entertaining the Commercial Manager of North American Oils, his wife might at least try to behave properly.

JANE. Why not slap my face while you're about it?
GEORGE. I just want you to realize . . .

(*The telephone rings.* JANE *picks up the receiver angrily*)

JANE (*into the telephone*) Hullo? . . . Oh, so it's you, Rupert . . . Well, I congratulate you. I never thought anyone could behave . . . What? . . . George did? . . . But why in heaven's name? (*She turns to George*) Did you tell Rupert he couldn't come?
GEORGE (*awkwardly*) As a matter of fact I did.
JANE. Why?
GEORGE. Because I'd—I'd heard he was a pretty poor type.
MERVYN. You're dead right.
JANE (*into the telephone*) George says you're a pretty poor type . . .
GEORGE. There's no point in . . .
JANE (*into the telephone*) Let him come and tell you himself . . . Right. Here he is. (*She holds the receiver to George*) You tell him.
GEORGE. What *now*?
MERVYN. Yes. Now. (*He crosses to George*) Tell him just where he gets off!

(GEORGE *thrusts the tool-box at* MERVYN *and nervously takes the receiver*)

GEORGE (*into the telephone*) Hullo? . . . Is that you, Rupert? . . . What? (*He looks at Jane and Mervyn*) He insulted me!

(MERVYN *puts down the tool-box and gives George a great nudge to encourage him*)

MERVYN. Go on. Don't let him get away with it.
GEORGE (*into the telephone; trying to sound fierce*) Listen, you! I've heard some pretty nasty things about you . . . Yes, I know your form. You go about having affairs with the wives of your very best friends.
JANE. What? (*She tears away the receiver from George*)
MERVYN (*into the telephone*) You unspeakable cad!

(MERVYN *snatches the receiver away from Jane*)

GEORGE (*into the telephone*) You're a menace to society.
MERVYN (*into the telephone*) You rotter. (*He holds the receiver in front of George and nudges him*)
GEORGE (*into the telephone*) You ought to be ashamed of yourself!
MERVYN (*into the telephone; very politely*) Good evening!

(MERVYN *quickly replaces the receiver*)

GEORGE (*proudly*) Did you hear what I said to him?
MERVYN. Let's only hope it registered.
JANE (*turning slowly*) You knew and you didn't say a thing?

GEORGE. Knew what?
JANE. Why not be honest and admit you couldn't care less?
GEORGE. What are you talking about?
JANE. All right then. Since you don't care I shall know what to do next time.

(JANE *exits to the kitchen*)

MERVYN. Now what's the matter?
GEORGE. I'm afraid she's realized that I've known about it all along.
MERVYN. You mean that she and Rupert . . .?
GEORGE. Oh well, you can't have everything your own way in life. It's my fault, you know, I must have been very dull. I now realize I've thought more about my business than about Jane. When I found out that she had been meeting another man in Town, my first reaction was fairly violent. I was certain there was nothing in it, but I still wanted to break everything in sight. One day I waited for her to come home. When she came in I could feel myself trembling. I was so wrought up I couldn't get a word out. She was looking even lovelier than usual. She asked me what was wrong. I said—I said that business wasn't too good. You see, I'd made my decision. I'd decided to let things go on as they were, rather than risk losing her for good and all. Besides I didn't think Rupert would last long. He's not the right man for her.
MERVYN. You know, if you're trying to lose Jane you're going the right way about it.
GEORGE. I know. When you were talking about women this afternoon I said to myself: "Now, there's a chap who knows what he's talking about." And I thought you could probably give me some advice.
MERVYN. I could?
GEORGE. Yes. You see, somehow I like you. That's why I felt I could trust you enough to tell you about things. Look, if you were me, what would you do?
MERVYN. If I were you?
GEORGE. Yes. If you felt your wife didn't love you any more, if you knew she was all set to fall flat for the first man who came along and knew his stuff—what would you do?
MERVYN. I don't quite know. I suppose I'd try to win her back.
GEORGE. Yes. But how?
MERVYN. To begin with I'd sometimes give in to her little whims.
GEORGE. But Jane has at least ten whims a day.
MERVYN. All the more opportunity. Take trouble over her. Make a fuss of her. And sometimes you can make love to her.
GEORGE. That's just what I wanted to hear. Do you think you could give me an idea or two. I've never known how to begin.

MERVYN. It's not hard. It's only a question of training. After a while it'll come natural. Suddenly you'll surprise yourself by saying the most entrancing things. If your imagination's not up to much you've got to skip through Shelley or take a dekko at Keats. If you find them on the slow side try Elinor Glyn.

GEORGE. What would you say to Jane if you were me?

MERVYN. I repeat—I simply don't know.

GEORGE. After what you said just now I should have thought you'd learned the knack.

MERVYN. One of the hardest things about making love to a woman is getting one's timing right.

GEORGE. Really.

MERVYN. Why not give her a bunch of flowers? And when you give them to her, say something nice—something that's sure to please her.

GEORGE. I see. But what should I say?

MERVYN. Whatever comes into your head. (*He crosses to the bookshelves*) You must work it out for yourself.

GEORGE (*following Mervyn*) I thought at least you'd try to help me.

(MERVYN *picks out a volume and hands it to George*)

MERVYN. Here, this should do you!

GEORGE (*reading the title*) "*Romeo and Juliet*." Do you think so? Don't I seem to . . .

MERVYN. This'll inspire you.

GEORGE (*opening the book and reading*) "Deny thy father and refuse thy name; or if thou wilt not, be but sworn my love."

MERVYN. No! Not that! (*He takes the book and reads*) "For stony limits cannot hold love out. And what love can do, that dares love attempt."

GEORGE. Don't you think that's a bit old-fashioned?

MERVYN. My dear fellow, it's only to give you some idea and get you in the right mood generally.

GEORGE (*taking the book and reading*) "Therefore thy kinsmen are not let to me . . ." If I mention her family there's bound to be a scene.

MERVYN. Then cut them out.

GEORGE. If only I could!

MERVYN (*taking the book and reading*) "Look thou but sweet, and I am proof against their enmity."

GEORGE. "Look thou but sweet." Yes I could use that.

MERVYN (*skimming through the book to find a suitable passage*) "Yet, wert thou as far as that vast shore wash'd with the furthest sea, I would adventure for such merchandise."

GEORGE (*not very convinced*) You don't think that's rather over-doing it?

MERVYN. There's no need to use the precise words, but it's just to give you the general idea. Now, look! When she comes in, you must move towards her. (*He moves towards George*) If the flowers bother you, put them down on the chair. (*He pretends to put a bunch of flowers on the chair* c) Then, take her gently by the hand, and get her to sit down.

GEORGE. Won't that make her sit on the flowers?

MERVYN. No. You pick up the flowers first. And when she's sitting down you kneel at her feet. (*He kneels*)

GEORGE. Couldn't I remain standing?

MERVYN. No. You'd look a perfect clot making love to a woman on your feet. Then you hand her the flowers and you say: "Look, darling! Here are some flowers I picked for you."

GEORGE. Did you have to scour all Shakespeare to think that one up?

MERVYN. Perhaps you can do better?

GEORGE. No, no. You carry on—by all means.

(MERVYN *gets up and stands behind the armchair* c)

MERVYN. At this stage you can begin to stroke her neck, put your cheek against hers, and you can say something along the general lines of the stuff we've read out. For instance, you might say: "I would have crossed the ocean to bring you back these flowers."

GEORGE. Since her garden's a mass of flowers at the moment, that sounds idiotic. (*He is most embarrassed*)

MERVYN. This is a very good one—I want to kiss you all over —from your little tiny toe right up to your golden hair and then right down again to the little tiny toe of your little tiny foot.

(JANE *enters from the kitchen while* MERVYN *is speaking and watches them. She bursts out laughing.* GEORGE *is highly embarrassed and smiles sheepishly*)

(*To Jane*) What are you laughing at? Have I said something funny?

GEORGE. Of course he hasn't—it's very beautiful. (*To Mervyn*) Keep her here for a bit. I'm off to find my hammer.

(GEORGE *crosses and exits to the kitchen*)

JANE. "The little tiny toe of your little tiny foot", indeed!

MERVYN (*disappointed*) Wouldn't you like that kind of thing said to you?

JANE. The idea's all right. It's just the words that are funny.

MERVYN. Jane, there's something I must tell you.

JANE (*suddenly turning and facing Mervyn*) There's something I must tell you. Please try to understand. George stopped caring for me, and I so wanted someone to love me and make a fuss of me, and Rupert came along and he flattered me . . .

MERVYN. You don't need to explain. It's only natural. And while we're on the subject I'd like . . .
JANE. George knew. And he didn't mind.
MERVYN. That's just the point, Jane—George didn't know a thing. That was all my fault.
JANE. Your fault?
MERVYN. I wanted to be alone with you, so when I heard there was another guest coming I pretended I knew him. I told some cock-and-bull story about being at daggers drawn and your husband put him off. And that's all there is to it.
JANE. And you've never even met Rupert?
MERVYN. I don't know him from Adam. Are you furious with me?

(JANE *hesitates. Then she smiles and puts her arm round Mervyn's neck*)

JANE. No. Of course not.
MERVYN. Jane, I've got something more to confess . . .

(JANE *cuts him short by kissing him*)

(*Deeply moved*) Jane!
JANE (*snuggling in his arms*) Isn't it sad we didn't meet years ago?
MERVYN. Is it?
JANE. Perhaps I'd be your wife by now.
MERVYN. And perhaps we'd have reached the same stage as you have with George.
JANE. Maybe. Maybe not.
MERVYN. Either way, we'll never know.
JANE (*slowly*) Unless we try it out. Marriage, I mean.
MERVYN. On approval for a couple of years?
JANE. Why not?
MERVYN. You've a husband, remember?
JANE. I doubt whether he'll mind. When he's in one of his moods he's always talking about a divorce.
MERVYN. A divorce! But do you think you care enough about me to face up to . . .
JANE. Yes, I do, and I won't care what mummy and daddy say.
MERVYN. Mummy and daddy—are they still . . .?
JANE. Oh, yes. Daddy's a retired General but won't accept the fact. He treats Mother as a rather incompetent A.D.C., me as a newly appointed Subaltern and George as his Batman.
MERVYN. He sounds delightful.
JANE. He's full of speeches about the Flag, the Regiment; and Duty comes first.
MERVYN. So it should—in the Army.
JANE. George and I see a tremendous lot of them.

MERVYN. Do you?
JANE. They insist on us dining with them at least twice a week and they come to us every Thursday.
MERVYN. Do they? Every Thursday?
JANE. Oh, yes. I'm sure they'll like you—eventually. But there is just one thing, you won't suggest a drink in front of daddy, will you?
MERVYN. Why ever not?
JANE. You see, he's a rabid teetotaller, won't allow a drop in the house.
MERVYN. You mean that three times a week . . .?
JANE. Oh, don't worry, there are plenty of soft drinks, or tea if you prefer it.
MERVYN. Tea! Poor George.
JANE. They're both perfect pets. You'll see for yourself.
MERVYN. I meant poor George losing all his family like this, in one fell swoop. You know divorce is a very serious step to take. You should think twice about rushing into . . .

(GEORGE *enters up* C, *carrying a bunch of flowers*)

MERVYN. Found your hammer?
GEORGE (*hiding the flowers behind his back*) Yes.
MERVYN. If you'll excuse me, I think I'll go out for a walk. See you later.

(MERVYN *exits up* C. JANE *moves towards the kitchen door.* GEORGE *hesitates, then puts his bunch on the chair* C, *crosses to* JANE *and takes her by the hand*)

GEORGE. Jane.
JANE. Yes?
GEORGE. You're looking pretty this evening.
JANE. Thank you.
GEORGE. Please sit down. (*He leads Jane to the chair* C)

(JANE *sits on the flowers and jumps up with a cry*)

JANE. Oh!
GEORGE. Sorry. (*He removes the flowers*) Now you can sit down.

(JANE *sits*)

(*He kneels at her feet and hands her the flowers*) I picked a few flowers for you.
JANE (*taking the bunch*) George, how sweet of you!
GEORGE. I'd have swum right out to sea to get them—just to make you happy.
JANE (*looking at him in amazement*) What?
GEORGE (*trying to get the right words*) What love can do—one daren't always attempt.
JANE. What's that?

GEORGE. Look thou but sweet, and I'll ask your parents to lunch.
JANE (*more and more confused*) What are you talking about?
GEORGE (*taking her in his arms*) Oh, my darling little Juliet.
JANE (*springing to her feet*) Juliet!
GEORGE (*rising*) I mean Jane.
JANE. Don't try to get out of it. You've given yourself away.
GEORGE. No, I haven't.
JANE. Yes, you have. You've got a girl-friend.
GEORGE. But, Jane . . .
JANE. You shut up! For three whole years you've taken me for granted. And when you do take notice again your big idea of romance is to tell me you love someone else. Here! Take your wretched flowers. (*She throws the flowers in his face.*)
GEORGE. You must let me explain.
JANE. There's no need for any explanation.
GEORGE (*moving to her*) But there is.
JANE. Get out of my sight.
GEORGE. Jane, please listen to me. (*He tries to take her hand*)

(MERVYN *appears outside the window up* LC)

JANE. Don't touch me, you beast!
GEORGE (*trying to seize hold of her*) I'll jolly well make you listen.
JANE (*shouting*) Let me go.

(JANE *pushes George into the chair* C *and exits to the kitchen.* MERVYN *has been standing outside the window, listening to their last few lines*)

MERVYN. What's going on?
GEORGE. What's going on? What's going on is that it just didn't work.
MERVYN (*coming into the room*) Why not?
GEORGE. I called her "Juliet" by mistake and now she's simply furious.
MERVYN. But, my dear man, that's excellent.
GEORGE. You think so?
MERVYN. I certainly do. If she'd taken it calmly I'd have said you hadn't a hope. But her getting in a rage is a sure proof of love.
GEORGE. Well, that's something. *Now* what should I do?
MERVYN. Carry right on. Why not try a new line of attack?
GEORGE. Got more tricks up your sleeve?
MERVYN. Why not smarten yourself up for dinner?
GEORGE. Smarten myself up? You mean put on a dinner jacket?
MERVYN. No—no. Haven't you got something that would make Jane look at you with a gleam in her eye?
GEORGE. Well, I've got a jolly nice dark brown worsted.

MERVYN. Haven't you got something gay and light-hearted?
GEORGE. I haven't got anything like that. There's only that outfit Jane insisted on buying me for the South of France, and I couldn't wear that.
MERVYN. My dear fellow, that's the very thing.
GEORGE. Do you think so?
MERVYN. Yes.
GEORGE. You do have some extraordinary ideas. How on earth is this going to help?
MERVYN. Wait and see!
GEORGE. No, I'm damned if I will.
MERVYN. If you ask for my advice, you should take it.
GEORGE. I shall look an awful fool.

(MERVYN *pushes* GEORGE *through the kitchen door and shuts it. A few seconds later* GEORGE *returns*)

Couldn't I wear the worsted?
MERVYN. No.

(GEORGE *exits to the kitchen.*
JANE, *in a rage, enters up* C)

JANE. Mervyn, do you know what I've just found out?
MERVYN. What?
JANE. George has been having an affair with another woman.
MERVYN. George has?
JANE. It really is too bad! When I always thought he was at least faithful to me.
MERVYN. The man has got some excuse.
JANE. Don't you try to stand up for him. His behaviour's positively monstrous. When I think of him coming hot-foot straight from another woman's arms—the whole idea's revolting.
MERVYN. Are you jealous?
JANE (*on edge*) Certainly not. In fact, I can't imagine why I even mentioned it. (*She puts her arms round Mervyn*) Besides, why should we bother?
MERVYN (*gently*) Jane, I wonder if we ought? When I think of George . . .
JANE. You're right. We must tell him straight away.
MERVYN. That's not quite what I meant.
JANE. What else can we do?
MERVYN. There must be some way out—without rushing things.
JANE. You'd stand for us being—doing—while I was still married to George?
MERVYN. Certainly not. But perhaps—just for a start . . .
JANE. Never.
MERVYN. It's going to be a ghastly shock for him.

JANE. I daresay. But when he knows that I've got the chance of starting a new life, of having children . . .

MERVYN. Children . . .!

JANE. Just one for a start.

MERVYN. You don't think we should travel around during our first years together?

JANE. No, I don't. We mustn't make the same mistake as I made with George. We began by saying we wouldn't have children for a while. Then we got to discussing them in the same breath as installing a new frig. And now the question doesn't even arise. No. We must have children right away.

MERVYN. I see your point. But we don't want to be rash, do we? I mean, supposing after a while you came to regret having married me. You might even feel remorseful.

JANE. Remorseful?

MERVYN. You might. And that's why I've got a proposal. Jane, why don't you put out a feeler to see if a reconciliation with George wouldn't still be possible. It might even be the best thing.

JANE. And what about you?

MERVYN. So far as I'm concerned I want to make sure you won't have forgotten all about me in a week's time.

JANE. Supposing I don't make it up with George?

MERVYN. Then you'll have nothing to lose. And if you still take me seriously and don't think I'm just a clown, we can get everything straightened out.

JANE. Oh, Mervyn! (*She flings her arms round Mervyn's neck and kisses him*)

(GEORGE *enters from the kitchen wearing his new clothes. He sees* JANE *and* MERVYN *locked in a passionate embrace*)

GEORGE. Oh!

(JANE *and* MERVYN *spring apart*)

Don't tell me this time you've taken a sleeping draught.

JANE } (*together*) { Well, yes, we . . .
MERVYN } { Well, no, but . . .

JANE. No, we haven't taken a sleeping draught. But we've decided to come clean.

MERVYN. Jane, are you mad? We've already arranged . . .

JANE. It's not worth while. I've put out feelers before now and it was no good. (*She turns to George*) You'd better know the truth. Mr Browne and I are in love.

GEORGE. Mr Browne and you?

JANE. You tell him, Mervyn.

MERVYN. Mrs Maxwell certainly has a quaint way of putting things . . .

JANE (*to George*) You've said time and again it was better to separate than to carry on as we were.

GEORGE. I did. But I don't quite see the connection.

JANE. Well, now it's settled. We shall get divorced. And I shall marry Mr Browne. Now you can sort it out between you. Excuse me.

(JANE *exits up* C. GEORGE *and* MERVYN *look awkwardly at each other*)

GEORGE. You want to marry my wife?

MERVYN. I realize you must be rather surprised. Even I . . .

GEORGE. But you haven't known each other twenty-four hours.

MERVYN. I know. I simply can't understand it.

GEORGE (*sitting on the sofa*) And I trusted you—I even confided in you.

MERVYN. Little did you know how much you hurt me—telling me all your troubles.

GEORGE. You've no idea how much you embarrassed me . . .

MERVYN. Now let me explain . . .

GEORGE. You can save your breath. Jane was dead right. And I've just had one more proof we'll never get on. What I can't understand is how she fell in love with you so quickly.

MERVYN. I made her believe I'd been her lover.

GEORGE. And she swallowed that?

MERVYN. Yes.

GEORGE. Well, I take off my hat to you. I've never even been able to make her believe I was her husband.

MERVYN. I only said it to tease her because she was so nasty to me.

GEORGE. Do you think you can make her happy?

MERVYN. I haven't even had time to think about it.

GEORGE. Do you really love her?

MERVYN. Strange as it may seem—I—er . . .

GEORGE. I'm asking you these questions because on first sight you don't seem cut out for marriage.

MERVYN. Nor on second sight either. That's why I'm so frightened.

GEORGE. Do you want to change your mind?

MERVYN. Well, no.

GEORGE. Very well—then I'm the one who'll have to go. (*He rises and calls*) Jane!

(JANE *enters up* C)

Jane—I just wanted to say good-bye.

MERVYN. Look here, you can't go off like that.

GEORGE. Better we should make a clean break and separate before we begin to hate each other. I'm leaving you both, and I wish you all the luck in the world. Good-bye, Jane.

JANE. Aren't you going to kiss me?

GEORGE. No reason why not. (*He kisses Jane*)

(JANE *brushes away a tear*)

JANE (*in a stifled voice*) Good-bye, George.
GEORGE. Good-bye, Jane. (*He looks at Mervyn*) Good-bye.

(GEORGE *moves towards the kitchen door.* MERVYN *dashes after him*)

MERVYN. There's no mad hurry, you know.
GEORGE (*turning*) You've won, and I hope I'm a good loser. Good luck!

(GEORGE *exits quickly to the kitchen*)

MERVYN. Mr Maxwell!

(JANE *bursts into tears*)

JANE (*sobbing*) At least we know where we stand.
MERVYN. We certainly do. You know I can't help feeling we've been slightly rash.

(JANE *flings herself into Mervyn's arms*)

JANE (*sobbing loudly*) We're going to be so happy together.
MERVYN. Of course we are—we seem to have got off to an awfully bad start, don't we?

(GEORGE *enters from the kitchen*)

GEORGE. Please forgive me for interrupting you. But there's one thing I should like to settle before I go. It's about this cottage. Jane's probably told you I loathe the country?
MERVYN. We've never discussed the matter.
JANE. George, we've hardly had time.
GEORGE. I daresay not. Well, this is the point. I bought this place to please her. I wanted to make one of her dreams come true. As a girl she'd always longed for a husband and children and a little cottage in the country. Well, her husband's off, and we've had no children . . .
JANE. Because *you* didn't want any.
GEORGE. That's beside the point. I hope you'll now have at least half a dozen.
MERVYN (*hastily*) Only one for a start.
GEORGE. You can decide that between you. We're discussing this cottage. Now I've no intention of keeping it on. But I believe Jane really loves this place. (*He turns to Mervyn*) So if you like I'll sell it you. What about it?
MERVYN. Well—er . . .
GEORGE. Good. I can make out a provisional contract right away. (*He crosses to the bookshelves* R)
MERVYN. There's no hurry. Can't we do all the legal stuff in London?

GEORGE. No. Let's settle it once and for all. Then we needn't even think about it again. (*He takes a writing-pad from the drawer*)

MERVYN. Doesn't this kind of thing have to be done by a solicitor?

GEORGE (*sitting in the chair* C) I'll make out a simple form of agreement. The solicitor can fill in the details, and you won't even need me there—far less embarrassing. (*He fumbles in his pockets, then turns to Jane*) Have you got my pen?

JANE. Isn't it in your coat?

GEORGE. I shouldn't be asking you if it was—would I?

JANE. You must have put it somewhere.

GEORGE. No, I didn't. I'm sure you had it the other day. Why can't you get yourself a pen? I can't keep a thing of my own in this place.

MERVYN. Here, take mine!

GEORGE (*feeling in his pocket*) Here it is! Would you believe it! (*He takes a fountain pen from his pocket*)

JANE. You had it all the time. And then you say I pinch things. (*She weeps*)

(GEORGE *straightens out his sheet of paper and writes with an air of finality*)

GEORGE. Right. Now. (*He reads aloud as he writes*) "I, the undersigned—George Maxwell do hereby acknowledge that I have sold my cottage known as 'My Dovecot' . . ."

MERVYN. Your Dovecot?

GEORGE. Yes, this cottage is called "My Dovecot".

MERVYN. Is it really?

GEORGE. "Situate near Little Grittenden near Dymchurch in the County of Kent to Mr Mervyn Browne—

GEORGE }
MERVYN } (*together*) Mervyn with a Y. Browne with an E.

GEORGE. —for the sum of . . ." What price shall we say?

MERVYN. I've no idea.

GEORGE. Of course I got it quite cheap. But I've made a number of improvements.

JANE (*still sniffing*) We had a bathroom put in and a new kitchen-sink unit, the shelf above the cooker for the saucepans and the thing for rubbish and the washing machine—that's not counting what we did ourselves. But I suppose we oughtn't to charge him for that? George, what do you think?

GEORGE. Certainly not. (*He turns to Mervyn*) Three thousand all right?

MERVYN. You know, I'm not madly keen on the country either.

GEORGE. You need say no more. I'll put an advertisement in the papers.

JANE (*bursting into tears*) When I think of all the trouble I took over the place.

MERVYN (*genuinely moved by her grief*) All right. If you really care that much for it. (*He turns to George*) Two thousand?

GEORGE. Three.

MERVYN. Two thousand five hundred.

GEORGE. Three.

MERVYN. Three.

GEORGE. Done.

JANE (*flinging her arm round George's neck*) Oh, thank you, George!

GEORGE (*gently detaching her*) You must thank this gentleman.

JANE (*embracing Mervyn*) Oh, thank you, Mervyn.

MERVYN. Don't mention it.

GEORGE. Well, that's that. You can settle the account later.

JANE (*to Mervyn*) Since we all want it over and done with why don't you give him a cheque?

MERVYN. What, right now?

JANE. Yes.

(MERVYN *takes out his cheque book and pen*)

GEORGE. Thank you very much. Wait just a second and I'll give you my lawyer's address. I'll write it on the back.

(GEORGE *writes down the address while* MERVYN *makes out the cheque*)

(*He rises*) There you are!

(GEORGE *and* MERVYN *exchange documents.* JANE *bursts into tears,* GEORGE *puts his arms round her in a brotherly way*)

Don't cry. It's not easy, I know. But you'll be surprised how quickly you forget. (*He turns desperately to Mervyn*) Look, you take her. You're better at this kind of thing than I am.

(GEORGE *hands Jane over to Mervyn*)

Well, I'll be going. (*He moves towards the door up* C)

MERVYN. Mr Maxwell, before you go, if it's any help to you in your oil business look up a man called Gerald Harker and mention my name.

GEORGE. Gerald Harker?

MERVYN. Yes. He's a great friend of mine. And he's the Commercial Manager of North American Oils Inc.

GEORGE. But I thought you were?

MERVYN (*laughing lightly*) I've never put a foot in the place!

JANE. Do you mean you're not the Commercial Manager of N.A.O.I.?

MERVYN. No. Mine is rather an unusual profession. That's why I so seldom discuss it.

JANE. What do you do?
MERVYN. If you come to think of it, every calling in life has its uses. When you come into the world, you require the services of a midwife. When you leave it—you do business with me.
JANE. You're not an Undertaker?
GEORGE. Undertaker! My God!
MERVYN. Mortician—please! We find the American term so much more felicitous.
JANE. Oh! Do you mean you wear a . . . (*She makes a gesture indicating a tall hat*)
MERVYN. Yes. Browne's for Burials. In the family from father to son since eighteen-twelve. Browne's have been Burying for Over a Century. And the ghastly thing is it's true.
JANE. But why on earth did you tell us you . . .?
MERVYN. Let me explain . . .
GEORGE. He can tell you all about it as soon as I've gone. And I'm off right now. Good-bye, Jane.

(GEORGE *and* JANE *exchange a long look*)

MERVYN (*awkwardly*) I expect you've still got a few things to say to each other. I'll leave you for a bit.

(MERVYN *exits up* C)

JANE. Undertaker! (*She sits on the sofa*)
GEORGE. It's a very dignified profession. Cheer up! (*He forces himself to be matter of fact*) You can come and collect your things from the flat when you feel like it. You've got a key. You'd better leave it with the hall porter. And you might bring up any stuff I've left down here while you're about it.
JANE (*crying*) Oh, George!
GEORGE. I think that's everything. If anyone had told me that I'd arrive here at eleven o'clock on a Friday evening a married man, and leave at eight-thirty on Saturday a bachelor, I just wouldn't have believed them.
JANE. Eleven o'clock on a Friday evening?
GEORGE. We were still a married couple last night, weren't we?
JANE. You arrived at eleven o'clock?
GEORGE. Yes, about. I left London just before nine.
JANE. But Cynthia rang me at a quarter to eleven.
GEORGE. So what?
JANE. So what! Do you realize I only took my sleeping draught just before she rang.
GEORGE. I don't quite see what you're getting at.
JANE. What I'm getting at is that in between a quarter to eleven when I took my sleeping draught and eleven o'clock when you arrived, there just wasn't time for two glorious hours.
GEORGE. Two glorious hours between eleven and quarter to?

JANE. Can't you understand? Heavens above! Look, George! Did you know that Mervyn Browne has never met Rupert?

GEORGE. But he knew him well.

JANE. I tell you he doesn't. He told you he did because he wanted to be alone with me.

GEORGE. Did he really?

JANE. It was the same with being Commercial Manager of N.A.O.I.

GEORGE. You mean he said that so he could be alone with you?

JANE. No. So you'd ask him to stay the weekend.

GEORGE. Well, I never!

JANE. There's not a word of truth in anything he says.

GEORGE. Do you realize he told me he'd made you believe you'd been lovers. Naturally I didn't ask for any details, but I thought it was preposterous at the time.

JANE. Utterly ridiculous! Did you believe his story about his car and the sleeping draught?

GEORGE. That part—yes, I did. Otherwise how can you explain the fact that he was lying down beside you?

JANE. Oh, yes. We'd better believe that one. I think it was probably the only true thing he said.

GEORGE (*sitting beside Jane on the sofa*) You just can't take the man seriously.

JANE. You certainly can't. What a fool I've been. George, do you really think we can't make a go of it?

GEORGE. It was you that said we wouldn't.

JANE. I never said anything of the kind.

GEORGE (*back to the old form*) I can assure you that only ten minutes ago you positively . . .

JANE (*suddenly*) George, hold me in your arms.

(GEORGE *takes Jane in his arms.* JANE *slips her arms under his coat*)

GEORGE. Ouch!

JANE. What's the matter?

GEORGE. Your nails are digging into my neck.

JANE. Sorry. That better?

GEORGE. Much.

JANE. You do look nice.

GEORGE. Do I?

JANE. Say something romantic.

GEORGE. I wish I could. But I can't think of anything to say.

JANE. Try to, George. Please.

GEORGE. Jane, I do love you.

JANE (*off again*) Then why were you unfaithful to me?

GEORGE. I've never been unfaith——

JANE. Liar!

GEORGE. I give you my word of honour.
JANE. Then who's Juliet?
GEORGE. You.
JANE. Me?
GEORGE. I wanted to find something really beautiful to say to you so Mr Browne advised me to get a few tips from Shakespeare. I wanted to be your Romeo.
JANE. So that was it.
GEORGE. Yes.
JANE (*putting her cheek against his*) You could be if you wanted to.
GEORGE. You don't think it's too late to start all over again?
JANE. Not if we start from scratch. Oh, George, I've had such a wonderful idea!
GEORGE. What?
JANE. Why don't we buy that yacht we saw for sale in Rye? Then we could take it to Cannes for your holiday. Think of sailing gently through the Mediterranean. Think of the warm nights and the Hunter's Moon softly filtering through the sails . . .
GEORGE. If you really want it, I suppose . . .
JANE. George, I've had another idea.
GEORGE. What's that?
JANE. Why don't we go and buy it right away?
GEORGE. What, now?
JANE. Why not? (*Hurriedly*) It was dirt cheap and the owner lives on board. We could collect a suitcase from the flat . . .
GEORGE. Honestly, Jane, it's not on. How do we know . . .?
JANE. George, I know it's just a whim. But you might give in to me once in a while.
GEORGE. A whim? Why didn't you say so before? If it's a whim then I'm all for it. Let's go! What are we waiting for? (*He rises*)
JANE (*rising*) Bless you, darling. (*She goes to the door up* C *and calls*) Mr Browne!

(MERVYN *enters up* C)

MERVYN. Yes?
JANE. Mr Browne, I'm afraid we've been taking an unfair advantage of your hospitality.
MERVYN. What?
JANE. My husband and I don't want to outstay our welcome.
MERVYN. You've made it up?
JANE. Yes. And as we said before, you are a clown.
MERVYN. I told you so.
JANE. But no woman should be allowed to monopolize you. There are so many others who need cheering up.
MERVYN. Happily, yes.

(JANE *holds out her hand*)

JANE. So, good-bye, Mr Browne.
MERVYN. You're leaving?
JANE. It's better that way.
MERVYN. Then, good-bye.
JANE. No ill will?
MERVYN (*kissing her hand*) No ill will.

(JANE *exits up* C)

GEORGE. Good-bye, Browne. I can't think why Jane wants to rush off like this. But you did advise me to give in to her whims once in a while.
MERVYN. You're absolutely right. Good-bye, Maxwell.

(*They shake hands*)

JANE (*off; calling*) Coming, Romeo?
GEORGE (*calling*) I'm with you.

(GEORGE *exits up* C. MERVYN *is left alone. He looks vaguely round the room. We hear the car starting up. Suddenly* MERVYN *rushes to the window up* LC)

MERVYN (*frantically*) Mr Maxwell! Mr Maxwell!
GEORGE (*off; calling*) Now what's wrong?
MERVYN. What about "My Dovecot"?
GEORGE. Keep it. I've already told you—I don't like the country.
MERVYN. But neither do I. Remember? I just can't abide the country. It gives me the creeps.

(*The sound of the car driving away is heard*)

(*He rushes to the door up* C *and calls*) Mr Maxwell! Mr Maxwell!

(*The sound of the car fades*)

(*He looks around the room. He tries out the chair* C *and inspects the chair* R *as if computing their value. He notices the bunch of flowers on the floor, picks it up, gazes dejectedly at it, puts it on the stool and stands looking sadly at the flowers*)

(*The telephone rings*)

(*He moves to the telephone and lifts the receiver. Into the telephone*) Hullo? ... Mrs Maxwell? ... She's not here ... Who's speaking? ... Her friend Cynthia. (*He perks up a little*) I've heard lots about you ... You want to know if you can come down tonight? ... I'm sure Jane would be delighted. Jane's often told me how attractive you are ... You're a blonde, aren't you? ... What? ... Brown hair and grey eyes? I'm wildly intrigued. Hold on one second, I'll go and ask her—she's in the bath. (*He pretends to knock on a bathroom door and ask* JANE, *imitating noises, etc. Into the telephone*) Hullo ... Jane says she'd be delighted ... What? ... Yes, I'm sure she needs someone to cheer her up. So do I, come to that . . . You'll be a mother to us both. (*He laughs gaily*) What do you mean— at your age? You're still young, aren't you? . . . Fifty-eight! (*He is appalled. The receiver drops from his hand on to the rest, which cuts him off. He picks up the receiver again and shakes it wildly*) Hullo! Operator . . . Don't cut me off . . . It was a London call . . . Hullo . . . No, I don't know what the number was. (*He looks at the receiver as if it were a poisonous reptile. In a voice of utter despair*) This is the end.

CURTAIN

# FURNITURE AND PROPERTY LIST

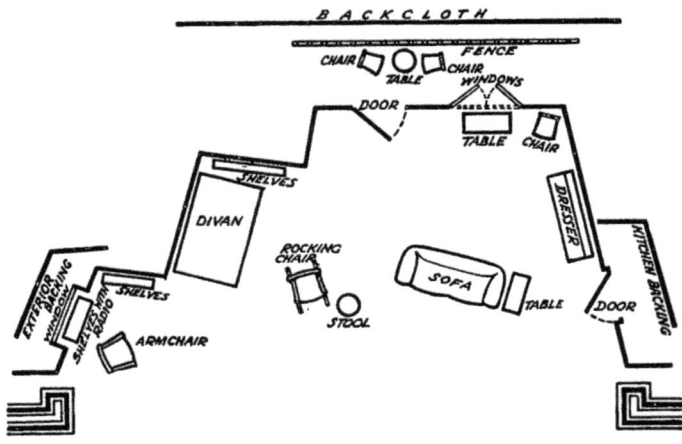

## ACT I

### Scene 1

*On stage*—Armchair (*down* R)
    Bookshelf (*down* R). *On it:* radio receiver, tray with 3 whisky glasses, decanter of sherry, bottle of yellow Chartreuse, bottle of brandy, jug of water, tumbler, 4 sherry glasses, 2 liqueur glasses
        *On shelves:* books, including copy of "Shakespeare"
Net and chintz curtains for window R
Bookshelves (R). *On them:* plant, ashtray
    *In them:* books, one on "Oils", ornaments
    *In drawers:* pad of notepaper
*On wall* R: oil lamp converted to electricity, cuckoo clock
Divan. *On it:* green linen cover, cushions, one with zip cover
Shelves (*above divan*). *On them:* table-lamp, ornaments
    *On shelves:* shells, books, magazines
*On wall* R: 4 modern pictures
*On wall above divan:* 4 theatrical "coloured" prints
Rocking chair (C)
Stool (L *of rocking chair*). *On it:* ashtray
Sofa. *On it:* cushions, library book
Table (L *of sofa*). *On it:* table-lamp, ashtray, matches, tray with jug of water, medicine bottle, tumbler, prescription
Chintz curtains for window up LC

Table (*up* LC). *On it:* vase of flowers
Upright chair (*up* L)
Dresser. *On it:* telephone, ashtray, box with cigarettes, table-lamp
    *On shelves:* decorative china, etc. 2 tumblers, cruet
    *In drawer:* loaded revolver, 2 table napkins, 4 knives, 2 forks, 2 table mats, 1 lb sausages
    Carpet and rugs on floor
    Light switch below door down L
    *On terrace:* white garden table, 2 chairs
Window curtains open
Window R closed
Window up LC open
Doors closed
Lamp L of sofa, on
Other lamps, off
Wireless on

*Off stage*—Suitcase (GEORGE)

*Personal*—JANE: watch
    GEORGE: watch

SCENE 2

Window curtains closed
Windows closed
Doors closed
Light fittings off

*Off stage*—Tray. *On it:* 3 coffee cups, saucers and spoons, bowl of sugar, pot of coffee, jug of milk (JANE)
    Packet of Aspro (JANE)

ACT II

SCENE 1

*Strike*—Revolver
    Coffee tray and cups
    Aspro
    Dirty glasses
    George's suitcase
    Tidy divan cover and cushions
Window curtains open
Window up LC open
Window R closed
Doors closed
Light fittings off

*Off stage*—Tray (JANE)
    Basket of cut bread, bowl of fruit (JANE)
    Shopping basket (GEORGE)

SCENE 2

*Strike*—Shopping basket
    Dirty glasses
    Everything from stool C
    Everything from garden table
*Set*—*On stool:* projector and slides
    *Up* C: projection screen
    *On sofa:* coffee cup and saucer
    *On rocking chair:* coffee cup and saucer

Move rocking chair R
Doors closed
Windows closed
Window curtains closed
Lights off
Projector on

*Off stage*—Marrow (JANE)

## ACT III

*Strike*—Projector, screen and slides
    Book from sofa
    Dirty glasses
*Set—On dresser:* tin tool-box with tools and hammer
    *On tray* R: 3 whisky glasses
Re-set chair C
Doors closed
Windows open
Window curtains open
Lights on

*Off stage*—Bunch of flowers (GEORGE)

*Personal*—GEORGE: fountain pen
      MERVYN: cheque book, fountain pen

# LIGHTING PLOT

Property Fittings Required—3 table-lamps, oil lamp in wall bracket, converted to electricity

Interior. A large cottage living-room. The same scene throughout

THE MAIN ACTING AREAS ARE—at a sofa LC, C, RC and at a divan R

THE APPARENT SOURCES OF LIGHT ARE—in daytime, windows R and up LC, and at night, table-lamps up R, L and LC and an oil lamp converted to electricity in a bracket on the wall R

ACT I   SCENE 1   Night

*To open:* Moonlight effect outside windows
Table-lamp LC, on
Other lamps, off

| | | |
|---|---|---|
| *Cue* 1 | JANE switches out table-lamp LC<br>*Snap out table-lamp LC*<br>*Snap out all on-stage lights* | (page 3) |
| *Cue* 2 | JANE lies on divan<br>*Effect of car headlamps sweeping across window* | (page 4) |
| *Cue* 3 | GEORGE switches on table-lamp LC<br>*Snap in table-lamp LC*<br>*Snap in covering lights* | (page 4) |
| *Cue* 4 | GEORGE switches on lights<br>*Snap in all fittings*<br>*Snap in on-stage lights* | (page 6) |
| *Cue* 5 | GEORGE switches off lights<br>*Snap out all fittings*<br>*Snap out on-stage lights* | (page 10) |
| *Cue* 6 | GEORGE: "Mr Browne! Really!"<br>BLACK-OUT. | (page 10) |

ACT I   SCENE 2   Morning

*To open:* The room dim
Fittings off
Bright sunshine effect outside door and window

| | | |
|---|---|---|
| *Cue* 7 | JANE opens window curtains<br>*Bring up on-stage lights* | (page 11) |

ACT II   SCENE 1

*To open:* Lights as at the end of the previous scene

| | | |
|---|---|---|
| *Cue* 8 | MERVYN: "Well—she didn't say 'no'."<br>BLACK-OUT. | (page 31) |

ACT II   SCENE 2

*To open:* The stage dim
Sunshine effect outside door and windows
Fittings off
Projector on

| | | |
|---|---|---|
| *Cue* 9 | GEORGE opens window curtains<br>*Bring up on-stage lights* | (page 34) |

ACT III   Evening

*To open:* All fittings on
Twilight effect outside windows and door

*No cues*

# EFFECTS PLOT

## ACT I
### Scene 1

| | | | |
|---|---|---|---|
| Cue | 1 | At rise of CURTAIN<br>*Music of "Someone to Watch Over Me" from wireless* | (page 1) |
| Cue | 2 | JANE zips divan cushion<br>*Telephone rings* | (page 1) |
| Cue | 3 | JANE switches off radio<br>*Stop radio music* | (page 1) |
| Cue | 4 | JANE drinks medicine<br>*Telephone rings* | (page 2) |
| Cue | 5 | JANE exits<br>*Cuckoo clock strikes 11* | (page 2) |
| Cue | 6 | JANE lies on divan<br>*Sound of car arriving and stopping* | (page 4) |
| Cue | 7 | GEORGE exits L<br>*Crash of saucepans* | (page 6) |

### Scene 2

| | | | |
|---|---|---|---|
| Cue | 8 | After rise of CURTAIN<br>*Cuckoo clock strikes 9* | (page 11) |
| Cue | 9 | Follows previous cue<br>*Telephone rings* | (page 11) |
| Cue | 10 | JANE: "Get your coat"<br>*Sound of a car starting* | (page 18) |

## ACT II
### Scene 1

| | | | |
|---|---|---|---|
| Cue | 11 | JANE: "Goodness gracious!"<br>*Sound of a car arriving and stopping* | (page 21) |

### Scene 2

*No cues*

## ACT III

| | | | |
|---|---|---|---|
| Cue | 12 | At rise of CURTAIN<br>*Music of "Mr Wonderful" from wireless* | (page 44) |
| Cue | 13 | MERVYN: ". . . wanted to say . . ."<br>*Sound of hammering* | (page 44) |
| Cue | 14 | JANE: "What's that?"<br>*The hammering ceases* | (page 44) |
| Cue | 15 | MERVYN switches off radio<br>*Stop radio music* | (page 45) |
| Cue | 16 | GEORGE: ". . . want you to realize . . ."<br>*Telephone rings* | (page 46) |
| Cue | 17 | GEORGE exits<br>*Sound of car starting up* | (page 62) |
| Cue | 18 | MERVYN: "It gives me the creeps"<br>*Sound of car driving away* | (page 62) |
| Cue | 19 | MERVYN picks up flowers<br>*Telephone rings* | (page 62) |

www.ingramcontent.com/pod-product-compliance
Ingram Content Group UK Ltd.
Pitfield, Milton Keynes, MK11 3LW, UK
UKHW021840210426
5322IPUK00022B/395